*A Brief History of*

**Death**

*Blackwell Brief Histories of*
# Religion

This series offers brief, accessible and lively accounts of key topics within theology and religion. Each volume presents both academic and general readers with a selected history of topics which have had a profound effect on religious and cultural life. The word 'history' is, therefore, understood in its broadest cultural and social sense. The volumes are based on serious scholarship but they are written engagingly and in terms readily understood by general readers.

### Published

*Alister E. McGrath* – A Brief History of Heaven
*G. R. Evans* – A Brief History of Heresy
*Tamara Sonn* – A Brief History of Islam
*Douglas J. Davies* – A Brief History of Death
*Lawrence S. Cunningham* – A Brief History of Saints

### Forthcoming

*Michael Banner* – A Brief History of Ethics
*Carter Lindberg* – A Brief History of Love
*Carter Lindberg* – A Brief History of Christianity
*Dana Robert* – A Brief History of Mission
*Philip Sheldrake* – A Brief History of Spirituality
*Kenneth Appold* – A Brief History of the Reformation
*Dennis D. Martin* – A Brief History of Monasticism
*Martha Himmelfarb* – A Brief History of the Apocalypse

# A Brief History of
# Death

DOUGLAS J. DAVIES

**Blackwell**
Publishing

BLACKWELL PUBLISHING
350 Main Street, Malden, MA 02148-5020, USA
108 Cowley Road, Oxford OX4 1JF, UK
550 Swanston Street, Carlton, Victoria 3053, Australia

First published 2005 by Blackwell Publishing Ltd

*Library of Congress Cataloging-in-Publication Data*

Davies, Douglas James.
    A brief history of death / Douglas Davies.
        p. cm. — (Blackwell brief histories of religion)
    Includes bibliographical references and index.
    ISBN 1-4051-0182-2 (hardback : alk. paper) — ISBN 1-4051-0183-0
    (pbk. : alk paper)
        1. Death—Social aspects. 2. Death—Religious aspects. 3. Death—
    Psychological aspects. 4. Death in art. I. Title. II. Series.

    HQ1073.D383 2005
    306.9—dc22

                                                        2004011683

A catalogue record for this title is available from the British Library.

Set in 10/12.5pt Meridien
by Graphicraft Limited, Hong Kong
Printed and bound in the United Kingdom
by TJ International, Padstow, Cornwall

For further information on
Blackwell Publishing, visit our website:
www.blackwellpublishing.com

# Contents

# Plates

# Preface

This book brings into brief compass a subject that touches practically every aspect of life. The inevitable interest we all have in death – whether voiced or silent – is, often, unlike the interest we possess in other subjects. This one is infused with emotion, whether that of the experience of bereavement or of its anticipation, or of the thought of our own mortality. This brief volume seeks to capture some of these moods as reflected within the kaleidoscope of the history, religion and culture of many societies. I have taken as a guide for inclusion the interest shown by generations of students and others in particular aspects of death covered in courses I have taught, especially at Nottingham and Durham Universities. My own background in both social anthropology, involving empirical studies, and theology, with its reflective concerns, will also be evident throughout the text.

Here I thank those who have hosted me in numerous places in the pursuit of my death research. The authorities responsible for Stockholm's Woodland Crematorium and Bordeaux Crematorium allowed me to photograph at their sites, so too with Harry Heyink and Walter Carpey who also met me at their Amsterdam exhibition. I thank Roger Arber for his welcome at

Golders Green Crematorium, as well as for his involvement in, and wider support of, my cremation research through the Golders Green Foundation and the Cremation Society of Great Britain. Professor W. Trutwin entertained me in Poland and took me on an unforgettable snow-covered New Year visit to Auschwitz, marked here through a photographed memorial. By complete contrast of context I recall several friends, especially Profs David Paulsen and David Whittaker and their welcome in Utah, reflected in the Memorial Day photograph. The Aberfan photograph recalls L. J. who helped dig amidst the catastrophe and, unspeaking, took me to see the memorial. Finally, I take this opportunity to express thanks to Blackthorne Records for permission to use Ewan McColl's evocatively instructive song 'The Joy of Living'.

Douglas J. Davies
Durham

# Chapter 1

# Journey Beyond

The history of death is a history of self-reflection. Who are we? Whence do we come, and whither go after death? If there is an afterlife, what is it like and how might we prepare for it? But if this life is the fullness of our time, how best might we live it, knowing we are going to die? For much of human history, popular myth and formal theology have rendered accounts of death's origin and life's destiny. Philosophers, too, add their tight reflections while, in recent times, the physical and social sciences have opened explanatory agendas of their own.

At the heart of death's history lie not only the emotion of grief and the breaking of bonds between each other and our place in this world but also the hope of answering the queries and resolving the injustices of a lifetime. To perfect life's obvious flaws and resolve the persistent search for the meaningfulness of things has been a constant feature of afterlife beliefs. Three of the most longstanding and influential accounts of mortality are those of Gilgamesh, Adam and Eve, and Jesus Christ. These we consider here, while later, in chapter 6, we will sketch some other myths of death's origin.

Even to read the Gilgamesh myth is to sense the intervening millennia simply drop away before its expression of human experience. This, itself, is an important lesson as we ponder a history of death in which it is tempting to divide time into eras and to argue for different kinds of consciousness of death in each. We will bear that in mind as we sketch some of the distinctive ways and changing fashions by which human beings have dealt both with death as an idea and with the dead as lost kin.

## Gilgamesh

The ancient Babylonian Epic of Gilgamesh presents a philosophical reflection upon the human condition set in mythical form. This narrative of human friendship describes the devotion of one man for another, emphasizes the ravages of separation caused by death, and ponders the very essence of human nature by asking how animal and divine features underlie humanity: themes that recur in many religious philosophies, not least in Judaism and Christianity.

The princely Gilgamesh, himself two-thirds god and one-third man, meets the heroic Enkidu, depicted as a man-animal, 'coated in hair like the god of the animals' (George, A. 1999: 5). After a fight they 'kissed each other and formed a friendship'; their bond of attachment is only strengthened through the adventures and conquests they achieve together as when they slew the Bull of Heaven and *Humbaba*, protector of the great cedar forest. Gilgamesh experiences and expresses deep emotion in association with these conquests and receives powerful visions in a 'dream house' built for him by Enkidu. The gods declare that one of this pair must die because of the conquests they have made, and Enkidu is chosen. He learns this in a disturbing dream and, weeping, addresses Gilgamesh – 'my brother, dear to me is my brother' – asking how he will never see him again.

After twelve days of sickness Enkidu dies. Then, 'at the very first glimmer of brightening dawn', Gilgamesh begins to mourn for his lost friend in a deep personal sorrow. 'Like a hired mourner-woman' he weeps and bitterly wails. In a repeated verse Gilgamesh tells how he did not 'surrender his body for burial until a maggot dropped from his nostril' (Line X 60). These terrifyingly descriptive experiences bear upon Gilgamesh, bringing to him a sense of his own mortality; he declares: 'I am afraid of death, so I wander the wild'. He goes in pursuit of those who may provide him with the secret of eternal life. Further adventures take him past the scorpion-man, guardian of the densely dark tunnel under a mountain, and he endures a twenty-four-hour journey of darkness into dazzling light. He crosses the waters of death, assisting the ferryman in the process and still rehearsing his grief to all. He learns how eternal life was once granted to his forefather Uta-napishti for having built a great boat and surviving the world-flood. Gilgamesh, too, is rewarded for having conquered the watery deeps by diving to obtain a rejuvenating plant, 'the Plant of Heartbeat', whose name is 'Old Man Grown Young'. Tragically, on his homeward journey, while he stops to bathe in a convenient pool, a serpent steals this source of eternal life. The snake sloughs its skin in a dramatic symbolic expression of renewed life, but Gilgamesh weeps, having lost the hope of such life for himself. Returning to the city of Uruk he can only point out to his boatman the great walls of his city, walls he had, himself, rebuilt and walls that, now, would have to be his only memorial.

This myth could have been written today, so freshly do its ancient themes touch the ongoing problems of love, loss, hope and the realistic acceptance of the way things are. Its urban context leaves us with a hero who has had to come to terms with the fact that his only eternity lies in his patronage of architecture. Its distinctive realism could easily be taken to validate some forms of today's secular way of life.

## Adam and Eve

While Gilgamesh's journey brought him home again a wiser, if more lonely man, the biblical Book of Genesis furnishes an account of death's origin that also begins a journey, but one that would extend beyond the original individuals into a myth and a history of a journeying and multiplying people that still possesses a vibrant echo in today's world of Israel. The Genesis myth of creation begins the biblical account of humanity with death as the outcome of disobedience to divine commands. God tells Adam and Eve not to eat the fruit of the tree of the knowledge of good and evil on the pain of death. It is in and through this divine–human relationship that they disobey and eat. God then drives Adam and Eve out of the delights of the Garden of Eden lest, as the text enigmatically and in an unfinished way puts it, they 'take also of the tree of life, and eat, and live for ever . . .' (Gen 3: 22). To know good and evil is one thing, but to know 'life' 'for ever' seems to be quite another. Adam must now work in sweated labour to wrest a living from the earth while Eve will suffer pain in child-bearing. God makes it clear to them that they have been made from the dust of the earth and that they will return to it in due course: 'you are dust, and to dust you shall return' (Gen 3: 19). As that story unfolds, for in the myth it takes Adam over nine hundred years to die and become dust, the pair set out upon an extensive journey, out from the Garden of Eden into the flawed world of hardship and pain.

Strangely, the death of Adam, as of all his sons, is simply stated in an entirely unproblematic way (Gen 5: 5). There is no grief here. While Gilgamesh deeply loved his friend Enkidu and mourned his death, all as part of his coming to accept his own mortality, the Genesis myth introduces the story of Adam's sons, Cain and Abel, and there is no sign of love between them. Indeed, in answer to God's question as to where Cain might be, Abel provided the world with his infamous, 'Am I my brother's keeper?' (Gen 4: 9). It is in this Cain and Abel episode that death as a tragic problem first enters the Bible, and it intrudes as fratricide. Cain was a farmer and Abel a shepherd. Both brought offerings to God, and God preferred that of the flock to that of the field. The divine preference, one that is simply stated and not explained, prompts anger in Cain who lures his brother into the field and kills him, and his blood 'cries from the ground' to the Lord. Accordingly, Cain is cursed to be a wanderer and fugitive upon the earth and is sent out on his own journey of destiny. Yet, even as God 'dressed' the naked Adam and Eve as he banished them from Eden (Genesis 3: 21), so he now 'marks' Cain for his protection as he sets him on his road to the future.

The offspring of these early fallen heroes engage in many wanderings in hostile environments as they seek the goal of a promised land. God decides to fix their life-span at 120 years before deciding to destroy the earth in a flood, itself a catastrophe of immense proportion involving much human death. Still, he saves Noah whose ark becomes, as it were, a drifting promised land of safety, albeit for a short period before, finally, God establishes a covenant with what is emerging as his chosen people. It is this covenant of divine–human collaboration, the guarantee of many descendants and the hope of a promised land, that undergirds the sense of destiny and immortality of much of the following Jewish history. When they try to settle around the Tower of Babel, a monument they build on their own initiative to stand as a marker of their hoped-for territory, God destroys it and sends them, once more, on their journeying quest, for there is to be no settlement apart from the divinely apportioned land.

It is tempting to ponder the emphasis Genesis places upon bricks, the building material in which the migrants so eagerly sought to invest – 'Come, let us make bricks and burn them thoroughly' (Gen 11: 3) – and to set the frustrated hope vested in them against the way Gilgamesh has to be satisfied with his own city walls. For the Babel migrants it is their offspring and descendants who will, ultimately, reach a destination which, itself, becomes the prime hope rather than some personal paradise after death. Indeed, for the greater part of the Hebrew Bible (the Old Testament as Christians call it), ideas of individual life after death are shadowy or non-existent.

## Death, Sin and Atonement

It was only some two hundred years before the time of Jesus of Nazareth – interpreted as the new Adam who is obedient to God – that some Jews began developing the idea of the resurrection of the dead, in an act of divine vindication of the righteous. It was an idea that ran alongside the notion of atonement, the belief that suffering could counteract the effect of sin and restore ruptured relations with God. Suffering in this life could serve an atoning function, while death itself, which was more of a process of dying than an instantaneous moment, also served to atone for sins. These ideas came together in the interpretation of the life of Jesus as a saving passion: suffering and death were interpreted as making atonement for the sins of all and of bringing into sharp profile a fulfilment of the divine covenant. The immensely popular film *The Passion of the Christ*, directed by Mel Gibson in 2004, brought to the screen perhaps the most extensive pictorial displays of Jesus' suffering and death ever witnessed in cinema.

## Resurrection-Transcendence

With Christianity the Jewish sense of atonement gains renewed vigour in the resurrection of Christ and in the belief that Christians – indeed perhaps all people – will rise again to face a judgement and a future destiny of eternal dimensions, less in a promised land than in a promised Kingdom of God. Belief both in the resurrection of Jesus and in the influence of the Holy Spirit created a community of diversely originating people. This was the prime meaning of the Christian gospel: the good news was that God had forgiven sins through the atonement of Jesus, had created a new integrated world-community through the divine Spirit and, perhaps best of all, had conquered death in Christ's resurrection. His resurrection would, in due course, be experienced in the resurrection of individual believers in the last days. In this myth of destiny, death and Christ's conquest of death are absolutely pivotal to the emerging religion. Though earliest Christianity may have conceived of the eternal future in terms of a restored earth, a second Eden, over the following centuries the Christian afterlife was, largely, interpreted in terms of a heavenly domain. Christian theology, iconography, patterns of worship, the very existence of Easter and its religious celebration, and funerary rites came to speak of human life as a journey through life to the heavenly city. This journey beyond has dominated Christian cultures ever since, with only a relatively few wishing to interpret 'eternal life' more as a quality of existence in the here and now rather than an anticipated there and then.

Most important, however, was the ritual of the repeated Last Supper. What had been the Jewish Passover meal became the Christian rite variously called the Mass, Eucharist, Holy Communion or Lord's Supper. Scriptural words combined with the basic act of eating bread and drinking wine to frame the fact of the death of Jesus. With the emergence of Christianity as a world religion death became an explicit ritual concern of much of humanity. This began with the martyrs, developed as the faith became the religion of the Roman Empire, became culturally dominant in Medieval Europe, was refocused by the dynamic Reformation and was exported to much of the rest of the world during Christianity's new missionary form adopted in the eighteenth century.

Christianity glorified death. Death was the outcome of sin, yet sin was destroyed by Christ's pure life outpoured in his atoning death. He died, yet his death was subjected to resurrection. Henceforth the cross would become the symbol within which these many ideas would become condensed and mutually influential.

The Mass announced all this on a daily basis. Similarly, to see cemeteries with graves marked by a cross is to see this history of death. Sites so marked in anticipation of resurrection share a strong family resemblance with the graves of both some Jews and most Muslims who, though the cross is no part of their saving theology, see destiny as lying beyond judgement and beyond the grave. All these traditions could trace elements of their anticipations to the early roots of Zoroastrianism, the ancient Persian religion expressing the human sense of morality, resurrection and post-mortem judgement.

## Release-Transcendence

Religions originating in India, by contrast, set less store either by this world or any similar perfected landscape of eternity. Hinduism, Buddhism and Sikhism took death to be part of the immense cycle of ongoing existence from which the vital self should and might be released. In time, and after many incarnations and strict observance of proper behaviour, that final release might be achieved. In classical Hindu tradition the funeral pyre served the function of a kind of reversed womb. As the mother's 'heat' prepared the foetus for life, and as the spirit came to it in the womb, so the heat of the pyre prepared the corpse for the freeing of the spirit from the cracked skull. The pyre was an altar, the cremation the last offering of the self to the deity. Transmigration lay ahead, for reincarnation or, ultimately, for the freedom of indescribable bliss. In these traditions the history of death is more the history of 'consciousness', of a person's essential identity and what we might call its 'journey beyond'.

## Self-Transcendence

Whether in the form of mythical narrative, theological dogma or philosophical reflection, death beliefs help explain life itself. They point to life's goals and possibilities while acknowledging its difficulties and pitfalls. One philosophical means of interpreting human capability lies in the idea of self-transcendence. This begins in the powerful human sense of discontent, the awareness that things are not as they should be: human existence is flawed. Broadly speaking, Eastern religiosity roots the flaw personally, in consciousness and human desire existing amidst an illusory domain of untruth. Salvation lies in enlightenment, in awakening to true insight. Such a perspective assumes a variety of doctrinal views in Zoroastrianism, Hinduism, Buddhism and Sikhism. Western traditions too, focused in Judaism, Christianity and Islam, echo this tendency of human nature to see its world as faulty and people as wicked, disobedient as they are to divine command. Yet, there remains a desire to rise above these faults, to escape the flawed nature of things, to transcend oneself. A more theological way of saying the same thing is to speak of salvation. Salvation lies in responding to the revelations of God, in the forgiveness of sin and in the living of a new kind of life of obedience or submission to the divine. Whether from the illusion towards enlightenment of Eastern thought or from the fall to redemption of Western theology, human beings are provided with a means of self-transcendence: they may become new.

It is precisely this movement into newness that characterizes the 'journey beyond'. For many, the facts of life lie in the knowledge that life is painful and, while options exist, there is little they can do to pursue available alternatives. Some, however, do set out upon the journey beyond; they wish to attain religious goals and, in the most general sense, they desire salvation. These may not only benefit themselves but also those who do not so eagerly espouse the more rigorous way. In many Buddhist cultures, for example, the monks who are on the dedicated path also advantage the laity. In return for supporting monks, lay Buddhists obtain that complex commodity of salvation called merit. In Christian worlds, too, the saints and martyrs, along with other religious leaders, have been thought of as sources of succour. One of the commitments of earliest Christianity that was revitalized through the Reformation was to remove any scale of difference between religious experts and ordinary believers. Individuals, male or female, were to take responsibility for themselves in responding to the divine call to faith and in living the ethical life. In terms of this chapter, each person was to 'journey beyond'.

But it is not only within the world of salvation religions that such a journey has been possible, though they highlight it. In many pre-literate societies opportunities existed for individuals to gain new visions of their world that might contextualize death. Through rites of passage into adulthood, parentage or old age or through initiations into secret societies or religious leadership individuals could gain a sense of change and difference. Visions could be acquired and dreams dreamed. Sometimes it is in the occasional rites of Shamanism, with the ritual expert undertaking a trance-induced mystical journey into the realm of spirits, that ordinary mortals gain a sense of wider possibilities. It is precisely this sense of change or difference that shares in the general idea of transcendence or the 'journey beyond'. Such experiences also feed into thoughts of death and the possibility of an afterlife.

## Hope and Faith

To understand such transcending journeys is to identify the powerful experience of passing from one level of understanding to another when 'ordinary' life is given the opportunity to embrace mystery, awe and wonder. Devotees may come to realize that life is, indeed, 'extraordinary'. The history of death is an influential example of this extraordinariness of experience, but one that embraces the human proclivity for adventure – for going beyond the familiar into unknown futures energized by human imagination. Religion, philosophy, science and political ideology, each in their own way, engage in processes of transcending, of moving from one level of knowing to another. To grasp a higher view of things than has existed before is amongst the most basic of human activities; it is the foundation and the reward of the human need to 'understand': where rational 'understanding' is also pervaded by emotional desires for a sense of depth of relationship with people and the world around us as well as for some form of increased control over and security within that world of people and things. Indeed, the experience of insight that accompanies such shifts in knowledge is very largely ignored in the human and social sciences. Its recognition in religious 'conversion' is seldom linked with experiences gained through education, discovery and life's joys and sorrows.

One key element of the emotional energy motivating the human search to know more about our world is the sense of hope – that attitude towards the future which anticipates greater knowledge and a wider explanatory vision. There is an optimism in hope that fosters human endeavour in a committed search for solutions to problems even when they may appear insoluble. Hope makes it more likely that individuals or societies will overcome adverse situations to survive today and be even more prepared to face adversity in the future. There is survival value in hope.

Hope in general and religious faith in particular are very closely related and may even fuse. When St Paul composed his Christian poetic analysis of love in the famous chapter thirteen of the First Letter to the Corinthians, he spoke of faith, hope and love almost in the same breath and, even though his exhorting conclusion is that 'the greatest of these is love', he can also argue that 'love hopes all things'. Much depends upon context for these shades of emphasis to emerge; in religious settings hope often appears as faith while in secular situations hope expresses the human desire to flourish and has, from the later twentieth century, often been expressed in terms of 'spirituality'. It is clear that both hope and faith are extremely similar aspects of life.

One incisive observation on the place of hope in life came from the anthropologist Bronislaw Malinowski who argued that it was the role of magic to 'ritualise man's optimism, to enhance his faith in the victory of hope over fear' (1974: 21). And what he said for magic can, in effect, apply to many aspects of religion in general in contexts where human optimism comes to a ritualized focus: optimism, faith and hope cohere in a cluster of survival values. This emphasis upon hope affords a necessary prelude to any account of the history of death precisely because death has been amongst the most powerful, if not the most powerful of all, challenges to human significance and destiny.

Hope underlies the human drive for meaning; it fuels the processes producing the sense of transcendence in life. The human being, self-conscious and aware of living in an uncertain world of risk and potential danger, has found it possible to face daily life and hardship because of this attitude of possibility and a sense that difficulty may be overcome. The very fact of human survival attests to the driving power and 'attitude of possibility' captured in the idea of hope. Hope frames action in the present with the intention that it will achieve a benefit in the future. Hope counteracts despair, that sense of impossibility that fosters inactivity and allows negativity to triumph.

But death is especially important because it furnishes a prime context in which human hope faces potential crisis, when the motivation for life may be checked. As we will see in chapter 2, the death of others is one of the prime moments in life when individuals are prone to a sense of loss of purpose and of the worthlessness of life: why carry on when those who make life worth while have gone? It is precisely at the time of bereavement that less-stricken members of society bring their sense of hope to bear upon the hopeless. It is through funeral ritual that a people tell their stories of the meaning of life and enact their rituals of transcendence. It is through social activity itself that hope is manifest through many forms, in myths, doctrine, religious rites and formal liturgies of churches or, indeed, in secular rituals. The agreed-upon conventions of life merge with the people and institutions of power in a society to present a picture of the world and of the reality of the universe itself within which death is but a part within a greater whole. The bereaved individual stands between two forces: on the one hand the biological facts of life present death as decay with the implication that life simply ends – it is a tale that is told; on the other hand the cultural facts of life present death as potent with its own significance. For the great majority of individuals, society triumphs and the bereaved comes to live an ongoing life of some purpose and fulfilment. Sometimes, however, individuals are not emotionally convinced by society's claims and persuasions; they may be heartbroken, or philosophically persuaded that life is, essentially, meaningless, with any claim to the contrary being false.

## To Be or Not To Be

This is likely to be one of the most demanding questions of the twenty-first century. As this book will show, the history of death is very largely one in which people have shared a belief in some sort of life after death. While individuals may have completely disbelieved in any such thing, it has been exceptional for any society not to have held to such a view. Amongst the major exceptions are societies following communist ideology, as we see in chapter 3. While countries such as Africa, India, South America and, to a large extent, the USA possess large numbers of people with strong traditional religious belief and are likely to maintain a variety of traditional, Hindu, Christian and Islamic views of life after death, the ongoing nature of secular thought in Europe and parts of the developed world is likely to shift the place of death within human experience. We will explore this, in particular, in chapters 4, 6 and 8.

## Traditional Futures

So, for much of the past, as probably for the majority in the present, death relates to human identity as only part of a world-view, for beliefs exist to lead people beyond death. Hope impels human identity and opposes death. Hope's underlying drive for meaning sees through an inadequate world to a higher vantage point and, in so doing, invokes ideas of change and mystery, of a sense of movement into new possibilities. Some other aspects of human life reinforce this conviction that better things may lie ahead. Religious reformations or revivals, for example, confer a sense of the truthfulness of religious belief and add an increased charge to their power. In a rather analogous way, for example, the experience of romantic love is one in which life and the world may seem to change, an experience not restricted to one historical period of any single culture as was once assumed (Jankowiak 1995). The role of dreams and visions, along with the powerful insight of some scientific discoveries and the transforming nature of religious conversion, may all reinforce the human conviction that life is mysterious and that individuals are, themselves, sites of change. It is precisely against this background of human life that death may be understood; it does not stand alone.

## The Uneasy Species

There is also a certain intriguing quality associated with transcendence and it affects death. Human beings, unlike all other creatures as far as we are aware, find fault not just with themselves but also with their world. At one level this is perfectly understandable, for many things in life are awkward and thwart obvious plans, but at another we are led to see a species often ill at ease with its natural environment. It wants things to be other than they are. Many myths explain this in terms of how drought or hunger first appeared or, indeed, how death appeared. *Homo sapiens*, the uneasy species, appears to be exploratory by nature. Its expansion from its earliest members, probably in Africa, has populated the globe with its many diverse environments and, to those concrete domains of forest, plains and ice and sand deserts it has added new environments of the mind – heavens, hells, paradises and staging posts to rebirth on earth. For religious believers these transcendent worlds are believed to exist and to have been revealed by the deities to their human followers. While for non-believers those worlds are the outcome of imagination, they remain of considerable significance as commentaries on belief and as maps of human experience, emotion and relationships. But, although death may have prompted such beliefs in 'traditional futures', it is not something that can simply be described, classified, and theorized into insignificance.

## Death Our Future

Death, unlike many philosophical and religious ideas, affects each one of us as we encounter the death of those we love, of those we like, of the famous who serve as imaginary friends, of our neighbours and of those we hate. Moreover, although death is our future, it often takes time for that realization to dawn upon us. Here, as in many parts of this book, I am forced to generalize, knowing how dangerous and misleading that can be; yet, to make as broad a commentary as possible I am going to assume that death faces us in four ways, as (a) personal grief, (b) the death of others, (c) personal death awareness and (d) our actual death. Each of us encounters these experiences in different ways and, often, in quite different sequences.

## Autobiographical History of Death

In broadest terms a person is likely to first encounter death as the 'death of others'. Children hear people say that someone has died; they will no longer be going about their life, but this makes little impact. It is much like a piece of general community information. Similarly, people 'die' on television and in film every day. This, too, is largely devoid of serious impact. Then someone dies in the family; if it is a distant relative the death may be almost like that of the 'death of others' except that, now, a family member to whom one is close shows a degree of emotion over the death. A child, for example, may be aware of its parent being upset at the death of the mother's sister, an aunt relatively distanced from the child. The emotion of grief in another becomes a learning experience. Yet, even that is relatively little preparation for the day when the child, perhaps now already adult and with children of his or her own, suffers the loss of parent, spouse or even of their own child. As we will see in chapter 2, loss varies in many ways but there is something about grief that adds a new dimension to a person's life experience. Many would agree that life before and after grief is different. Even individuals who spend much of their life working with bereaved people or with the dead, as with funeral directors or priests, report how surprised they were when they were, themselves, bereaved. Such loss cannot be anticipated; no 'training' or 'preparation' is possible. Yet, even this kind of experience may be differentiated from what I have loosely called 'personal death awareness', a term describing that moment or period when an individual gains some degree of insight into the fact that they, too, will die. This kind of intimation of mortality exists as a spectrum, from a relatively light sense that what has just befallen someone one loves will, too, happen to oneself, through to the knowledge that one has a terminal disease and faces death soon. For some people the sense of 'personal death awareness' may come with age, especially old age, and is not perceived as some terrible problem. For others, often in middle age, it emerges in the mind as a novel sense of personal awareness unlike anything experienced before, and may or may not be disturbing. These varied responses will be pursued in more detail in chapter 2 and are pinpointed here to emphasize that the history of death embraces the innumerable histories of millions of personal biographies whose differences we can but note and whose similarities we hope might be broadly identified. As to death itself, but little can be said since it is a personal experience even though the dying individual may have others with them at the time. To this we return in chapter 7.

## Methods of Approach

Although what we have said so far has not been concerned with questions of distinctive methods of approaching our topic, it is worth drawing attention to the varied contributions made by particular academic disciplines to the study of death. Historical approaches trace changing attitudes towards death and in a very obvious sense present various 'histories of death'. Philippe Ariès is one of the best known and his analysis of death in European societies took the form of broad brush strokes, starting with death viewed as something natural and inevitable; this he described as 'tame death'. Then, from the twelfth century he refers to a long period when death became more individual before, in the eighteenth century, we became increasingly interested in the death of other people rather than of ourselves. As for the twentieth century, he saw that as a time when death became something 'unnameable' (1974). His broad survey is invaluable but always needs to be complemented by detailed analyses of particular countries as, for example, in John Wolffe's study of patterns of grieving in Great Britain in the nineteenth and twentieth centuries (2000). He showed how the deaths and funerals of famous solders, politicians and royalty affected the nation and helped frame the experience of ordinary individuals in their own domestic grief.

Philosophical approaches to death tend to reflect their own cultural background to a great extent and argue over the ways in which human self-consciousness can or should respond to the fact of death. Martin Heidegger (1889–1976), for example, analyses what effect the fact of the death of others and of our awareness that we, too, will die have upon our own attitude to life (1962). We can, indeed, come to live creatively, knowing that some part of our potential to do and achieve things is likely to be cut short. That kind of positive search for a framework for viewing death was opposed by Jean Paul Sartre who could not see that death could help provide any meaning for life (1956). In many ways death simply enhances his view that life is absurd. Life and death remain beyond human control and it is, for example, only in suicide that an individual may attempt to bring some control to it. Yet others think that a kind of transcendence over death is possible through philosophical argument (Metzger 1973).

Theological views of death provide one of the most extensive avenues of approach, largely because religions have provided the major means for dealing with death in human societies. Each major religion of the world possesses its own set of theologies or formal reflections upon the idea of the divine and of divine–human relationships. The whole issue of death-conquest has been a dominant concern in Christianity, with its notion of the resurrection from the dead, as also in parts of Judaism and in Islam. Hinduism, Buddhism and Sikhism have favoured some aspect of the transmigration of the soul, perhaps involving a reincarnation on the basis of meritorious moral achievement and anticipating some final release of the life-force. Earlier still, Zoroastrianism in Persia and the ancient religions of Egypt and Babylon possessed their own reflections on the destiny of the soul after death. The history of the theology of death is also intimately bound up with death rituals for, in religions, death is not simply or even primarily a question of philosophical reflection but of ritual action and of relating wider experiences of worship to the specific case of death. Within the theological method, then, the history of death also becomes the history of death ritual, something we will touch upon in chapter 5.

Anthropology and sociology have contributed a great deal to the history of death in two major ways. Through detailed studies of pre-literate peoples new information has come to light on how societies without written histories have dealt with death and, then, through the comparative method they have identified some common features of mourning and funerary rites and have offered some compelling theories for interpreting them. In particular, these social sciences have shown how individual identity relates to wider society, including the realms of the ancestors and deities, and how people's identities are changed through the death of each member of society. These issues are explored in some detail in chapter 3. Occasionally anthropologists make more directly philosophical observations, as when Edmund Leach argued that in traditional oppositions and associations between night and day and life and death we see 'religion tricking us into thinking of death as the night time and so persuading us that non-repetitive events are really repetitive' (1961: 126).

Psychology has focused much more upon individuals and the inner dynamics of personal identity in relation to death. A major concern has been with the way children become attached to their parents and later to other people and then with the way we all cope with the loss of that attachment that comes with bereavement. Grief, as the condition of loss of attachment, has been very extensively studied, as we shall see in chapter 2. Another aspect of the psychology of death concerns the fear of death but this, as chapter 7 shows, brings psychology into close relationship with other social sciences as well as with theology and philosophy in the very difficult task of seeing how different kinds of influences are at work in different societies.

Humanist and secular views of death will also be given appropriate attention throughout the book and while these are not what might be regarded as distinct academic methods of study they are closely related to numerous disciplines and are important as views of contemporary life. This will become especially apparent in chapter 4's consideration of ecology, chapter 6 on memory and in the final chapter's reflection on the future of death. Other approaches appearing throughout these chapters include those of art, music, literature and architecture, all as expressions of cultural creativity and the human engagement with death.

## Words Against Death

So it is that history, philosophy and theology, anthropology, sociology and psychology, as well as artistic, musical and architectural studies all play a double part in our book. At one level they allow us to take a slightly distanced position, to stand back – as it were – from death and to see how we might seek to understand our mortality. But, at another level, these disciplines are, themselves, a human response to death, allowing individuals to approach and grapple with one of the most basic issues of all. Depending upon an individual's intellectual outlook and belief, one or other of these approaches may come to provide the bedrock for an understanding of life and death. Such theories provide what I call 'words against death', a phrase that I have used as a basis for an earlier book, *Death, Ritual and Belief* (Davies 2002). In the following chapters, especially chapter 4, I will use this phrase as a shorthand description of the way human beings use language so as not to let death have the last word. As self-conscious, language-using and language-creative agents, human beings deploy their prime tool – language – to engage with death: often it is deployed as if it were a weapon against an enemy. Occasionally, however, the words seem to be friendly and to welcome death, and that, too, must not be ignored.

## Myth Again

While there is no single avenue to be preferred above all others in approaching the history of death, it is worth highlighting the fact that for much of human history death has been understood through myth. As we began this chapter with myth so, too, we end by returning to stories that explain it in terms of human emotion and social values. Myth resembles formal academic theories since all are but the creative outcome of human grappling with basic life issues. The earliest written forms of Gilgamesh probably belong to as far before the time of Christ as we now live after it, yet, across that four-thousand-year span, the themes of friendship, love, attachment, loss, the intimation of mortality, the desire for an eternal life and the realization that it may only come about in our earth-bound memorials are as real as ever. While Babylon's Gilgamesh is not a widely known story, myths and theories focused on the soul as something distinct from the body, an idea that took a very influential form in Greek philosophy, did become deeply influential in developing views of the afterlife. Much could be said about ancient Greek journeyings of the dead, as in 'The Book of the Dead' – Book 11 of Homer's *Odyssey* – in which Odysseus is set on his travelling adventure amidst many dangers and comes to the land of the dead. There the spirits of the dead flock around him, making clamorous noise and displaying the many forms their death had taken. Odysseus has his own death prophesied – 'far away from the sea, a gentle death . . . You will die peacefully in old age, surrounded by a prosperous people' (Homer 1991, 11: 135). Here, too, he encounters many of the great ones of his mythical world as well as dead friends and his mother who had died after he had left home. She tells him that it was her heart, broken in longing for him, her adventuring son, that had caused her death. There is nothing attractive about this shadowy afterlife whose inhabitants can still wish, as did Elpenor, Odysseus's travelling companion, to have his body burned and his ashes placed in a mound marked by his oar: Elpenor's accidental death from falling from a roof under the influence of an alcoholic hangover had left him dead but unburied as his companions left in haste.

Similar Greek ideas gained an even more influential basis in Plato who combined philosophical dialogues with mythical stories to give substance to the idea of the immortality of the soul. In Plato's *Republic*, for example, he argues for the immortality of the soul on the basis that not even immorality can destroy it (Plato 1974: 447–55). He develops his point through the myth of a hero figure – Er – who apparently dies in battle but who gains what would, today, be called a near-death experience. Though apparently dead in battle, his uncorrupted body is carried home and, fortunately, he awakens while on his funeral pyre and tells of his journey to a 'wonderfully strange place' where judges sit with two chasms set above and two below them. Souls pass up and down, some coming from their thousand-year underground journey of suffering and some from the delights of heaven above. They have the opportunity to live again in animal or human bodies of their choice. And according to their nature and virtue they do so. Ajax, for example, chose to be a lion because he had been so disappointed in the outcome of his human life and had committed suicide. Similarly Agamemnon, formerly murdered by his wife, Clytemnestra, became an eagle.

Beyond Greece, the idea of an eternal soul was also significant in ancient Persian, Egyptian and Indian religions and there are real possibilities that the Greeks were influenced by those perspectives. But it is not necessary to seek only for elements of historic linkage between cultures as far as souls are concerned, for most societies have developed their own sense of a life-force that continues after the body has died. This relates, for example, to many East Asian and African societies in which the ancestors play a significant role in society and in which funeral rites are the very means of conducting the soul on its journey beyond this world to the allied but different world of the dead. But, not all societies have held strong beliefs in an afterlife; indeed, Gilgamesh with his this-worldly realism contrasts markedly with Egypt's extensive architecture, priesthoods and theology of the afterlife. Some, as with Judaism, have even managed to combine the two and have changed with time. Today, much is changing as people interpret the world in increasingly diverse ways, and such changes affect the way we approach death.

# Chapter 2

# Parting's Sweet Sorrow

If Gilgamesh takes us to the earliest days of written accounts of human grief, the mummies of Chile take us even further back in their ritual treatment of the dead. From approximately 5000 BC the coastal Chinchorro people of what we now call Chile not only mummified their dead but also kept them for a period amidst the living. Possessing no written language, it is impossible to know what these practices meant, yet, two thousand years before the Egyptians began to mummify their dead, these early fisher communities along the Pacific Ocean did appear to have mummified all members of their society. Whatever sense of parting there may have been, the living retained the bodies of the dead, including infants below one year of age, giving them stylized masks as face coverings. And this in communities where, once the first year of high mortality rate is ignored, the average life expectancy was about 24, with most living between 15 and 30 years of age, but with some exceeding 40 years. In what were relatively small communities of what we would now consider young people it seems as though the group was extended by the inclusion of the dead.

These mummies gave anthropologist Bernardo Arriaza, who helped excavate them, both 'a feeling of continuity with the past' and a 'realization that all humans, past and present, share the suffering cause by the loss of a loved one' (Arriaza 1995: xiii). As he wondered just what 'emotions the Chinchorros experienced when someone in their group died' so, too, in the remainder of this chapter we approach the issue of loss and grief by exploring death's double face which, for the larger part of human history, has looked grievingly back on those left behind just as it turns hopefully to some ultimate destiny. We do this by employing both psychology and theology as ways of interpreting human experience and life's meaning, for death not only fractures our relationships with others and triggers grief, but also raises the question of how the way life is lived determines its meaning and ultimate significance. This is especially important for the large sweep of human cultures that posit a life after death based upon the moral path followed on earth.

## Relationships, Death and Destiny

It is through human relationships that we come to a sense of our identity and through their loss that we come to know grief. In traditional terms, it has also been through membership in religious groups possessing some relationship with deity that people have gained a sense of salvation or have feared damnation if that bond breaks. Control of the afterlife has typified many religious cultures and empowered its gatekeepers. Those who held a true faith and practised it according to prescribed forms would obtain benefits in life after death. In the early centuries of Christianity, when doctrine was being established, creeds came to be particularly important as formulations of accurate belief and as means of identifying group members. The creed of fourth-century St Athanasius, important for Catholic and some Protestant churches, begins thus in the version in Anglicanism's *Book of Common Prayer*:

> 'Whosoever will be saved: before all things it is necessary that he hold the Catholic Faith. Which Faith except every one do not keep whole and undefiled: without doubt he shall perish everlastingly'

This very strong language proclaims an 'anathema', a formal declaration on the state of persons who do not believe certain doctrinal statements expressing ultimate religious truth. This state of suspension or curse may even pass into formal exclusion through the ritual of excommunication conducted, traditionally, by a bishop with twelve priests, all with candles thrown to the ground when the excommunication was enacted. The rise of strong rituals associated with the sacraments of the Catholic Church involved a correspondingly high degree of control by priests of their people. Confession and absolution lay at the heart of religious discipline and of obedience to the authority of the church. The justification for this stance, derived from the words of Jesus spoken to his disciple Peter, became a charter for Peter's successors: it proclaimed, 'I will give you the keys of the kingdom of heaven and whatever you bind on earth shall be bound in heaven, and whatever you loose on earth shall be loosed in heaven' (Matthew 16: 19). Error in doctrine and practice could even be sought out as, for example, in the witchcraft hunts of the sixteenth and seventeenth centuries when those who were reckoned to have made a pact with the devil were tried and many killed. Their death would, doubtless, benefit them in the ultimate salvation of their souls. In this sense the history of death in that period of European history cannot be divorced from the history of church power and its use of the idea of true doctrine as a control over people's earthly and heavenly destiny. This is very clear in the Catholic practice of the

Last Rites by which dying people were strengthened for their journey into and through death.

## Family Bonds

Churches have also validated membership in society at large through, for example, marriage rites. Indeed, we can hardly over-emphasize the power of families in framing the deeply implicit emotional and unvoiced moods of belonging that merge with the explicit rational view of who we are in forging our sense of identity and destiny. Cultures that span millennia often promise an eternal community by conferring a complexity and multi-layered nature upon individuals that makes each person a minor miracle of existence. The stability and size of a society affect identity and the nature of our belonging to it, since those living their whole life in a small village, knowing only dozens of people, are unlikely to possess the same sense of self as those whose mobile lives bring them into contact with hundreds or even thousands of people over their lifetime.

In recent centuries marriage has been a praised and prized institution of most western Christian societies and, contrary to the general statement of wedding rites that the bond was 'til death us do part', most churches spoke as though heaven would be a place of continued partnership. Expressions of grief often alluded to heavenly reunions, as do innumerable gravestone in-scriptions. In modern, couple-companionate, society the stronger the idea of romantic love and mutual devotion the stronger became the sorrow of parting, albeit only for a while. By the beginning of the twenty-first century, however, many post-Christian western societies find marriage for life increasingly uncommon. People speak of serial monogamy, while divorce wit-nesses to the rupturing of relationships during increasingly lengthy lives. Indeed, the very thought of having to spend the whole of one's earthly life, let alone eternity, with one's first partner does not attract universal support. This example indicates something of how the history of death parallels the history of human relationships.

## Hell, Life and Work

Other changes have also affected ideas of eternity, none more so than hell. For centuries the idea of hell was sustained by Catholic and Protestant theology, reinforcing the doctrines of Christianity and helping to uphold social values. Hell threatened the wicked, while the doctrine of purgatory taught of a state in which souls would be morally improved for their final meeting with God. This ultimate promise of heaven helped provide a structure for practices of prayer and penitence and it is, for example, difficult to think of medieval Christianity without reference to the death-threat overhanging the afterlife despite the formal doctrines of grace, love and forgiveness. While one consequence of the Reformation and Protestant Christianity was a belief that God's chosen ones would escape purgatory to enjoy the heavenly pleasures of the worship of God, this did not always remove a sense of anxiety over death and the afterlife, as the Protestant use of the idea of predestination reveals.

Protestants of the Reformed tradition, typified by John Calvin (1509–64), held to the doctrine of double predestination, according to which God had established an eternal decree dividing humanity into the saved and the damned. Nothing could change one's status and no individual could know for a fact to which group they belonged. For dedicated believers this was a problematic tension. The way out of this doctrinal dissonance was described by the sociologist Max Weber as the Protestant Ethic, a scheme that united both theological and ethical aspects of life. On the one hand people argued theologically that God blessed those who were his: he caused their life activities to flourish. On the other, they sought to live dedicated lives, wasting neither time nor money, and this ensured that they did flourish. These two strands of thought, though not formally grounded in the logic of the doctrine of predestination, were brought together in a way that satisfied people. Despite many criticisms, some see this cluster of ideas as the basis for the rise of capitalism in western Europe, especially in the Netherlands. In this tangential sense the history of the fear of death also embraced, to some degree at least, the history of commerce and social development. As the twenty-first century begins, another version of the 'divine blessing' attitude towards life has become incredibly powerful amongst Pentecostal and some Charismatic Christians, especially in South America, through what is called the 'prosperity gospel'. This works quite apart from any belief in double predestination and correlates more closely with a belief in God's triumph over death in Christ's resurrection and his desire that believers should also triumph over the difficulties of their life, including relative economic poverty, prior to their future life in heaven quite devoid of trouble and, certainly, quite apart from any period in purgatory.

## Secular Ethics and Loss

Although, by contrast, many in Europe and elsewhere live by a much more secular world-view, they also find that identity is entwined with work and death. The rapid rise of secular ethics as a basis for moral decision making and life in today's complex world has, to a degree, replaced theology as a way of understanding the human condition. One secular version of the Protestant Ethic is evident in work-obsessed individuals who offer an instructive example of the way attitudes to death, work and life interact. It is not uncommon for such individuals to focus most of their life-energy on work and achievement, quite devoid of any expectation of eternal reward, but as an important way of establishing their sense of identity and meaningfulness in life. Then some crisis – a close bereavement or a serious personal illness – stops them in their tracks and triggers a reappraisal of life. Often it is the importance of the quality of time for relationships with others that now dawns on them; indeed, the very idea of 'quality time' and the 'quality of life' is thrown into sharp relief by death or the threat of death.

The interconnectedness of identity, work and relationships makes it possible to speak of the loss of a wide variety of 'things' as a kind of 'bereavement'. Enforced unemployment, along with some kinds of divorce following the 'death' of a marriage, has led some to liken these experiences to grief reactions (Burns 1989). Yet other life experiences such as the loss of a body-part through accident or illness, the death of a pet, retirement from an occupation that has largely defined a person's sense of self or even ageing and the 'loss' of youth are all open to interpretation as bereavement, with grief following the loss. For many who encounter the severe loss of a close partner or relative, however, these examples pale into insignificance.

## Freud and Bowlby

Viewing grief as a major human response to loss, psychologists have been influential in developing theories to account for human attitudes to death. Sigmund Freud, founder of psychoanalysis, viewed death as rooted in a human desire to return to the organic matter out of which we all emerged, and this despite the fact that individuals sense their own immortality (1920). Though Freud thought it impossible for people to imagine their own death he, nevertheless, pursued the idea of the 'death instinct' or *thanatos* as he called it (*thanatos* is the Greek for 'death'). This he took to be a negative and essentially destructive force forever struggling with human creativity and the desire for life.

This scheme of the forces of death and life is more balanced in John Bowlby's important researches on death which, while acknowledging the internal dynamics of our attitudes to those we love, also emphasizes the nature of the relationship between people and the support we may obtain in grief (1979). Bowlby began with the way in which human babies, not unlike young monkeys, clung to their mothers and displayed degrees of distress and apathy when separated from them. By extension he showed how grief at the loss of a support figure through death resembles other losses of supports in life. Over time a bereaved individual comes to adjust to the absence of the once crucial support and finds it in others. If someone continues to dwell upon the memory and image of their former life-focus they become less well adapted to life and continue in a pathological state.

## Grief-Stages

Many psychiatrists have stressed the relative importance both of the inner forces of self-identity and the outer networks that embrace the bereaved. This is important because people bring to bereavement many variables, including the quality of prior relationships and state of health. One of the most popular approaches to loss came in the well-known study of Elisabeth Kübler-Ross. It is interesting not only because of the actual substance of her work but because of the use to which others have put it. Her book *On Death and Dying* (1989 [1969]) needs approaching with caution on this second count because it has often been read and utilized uncritically. The book is an account of how a group of terminally ill people at an American university teaching hospital responded to being told they were going to die soon. She suggested a set of five responses, viz., (i) denial and isolation, (ii) anger, (iii) bargaining, (iv) depression and (v) acceptance. Other psychiatrists have offered different arrangements, and these have often been taken up by other professionals, as when Yorick Spiegel, a pastoral theologian, went so far as to relate four stages to a time period following bereavement: an immediate stage of shock lasting a few hours, a 'postimmediate' stage of three to seven days much under local cultural control, a transitional phase of up to three months, and a re-patterning of life taking people up to six months after bereavement (1977).

## Fixing the Unfixable

An unfortunate consequence of Kübler-Ross's work was that many turned these responses of the terminally ill into relatively fixed stages of grief in bereaved people. What started out as the response of those pondering their own death was turned into a set of stages of grief for people suffering the loss of loved ones. This reapplication is itself a telling marker in the history of death, for Kübler-Ross became popular just when death was becoming increasingly professionalized and less domestic, happening more to the increasingly old than to the young. I suggest that from the 1960s people in western, urban, societies were becoming increasingly less familiar with death and, in the absence of personal experience, some, especially literate and normally well-informed professional people, found this kind of technical study of real use in filling an experience-gap in their lives. While a degree of information is always useful it can, however, become problematic if individuals are told that there are stages of grief that they 'should' experience while, in fact, they do not do so. The variability of human response makes any formula hazardous. It is wiser, perhaps, to think of these and any other responses to the loss of people as more like colours and patterns in a kaleidoscope that vary from day to day even though they may all be present but not central to view at any one moment.

## Helplessness

Another approach to loss and grief, that of Wolfgang and Margaret Stroebe (1987), focuses on the support networks that maintain most of us in a relatively healthy state most of the time. Though many experience balanced and complementary relationships, some individuals are very dependent upon an extremely narrow support-base as, for example, where a wife did not go to work and experience a distinct network there. Her husband may have taken most major decisions, including economic ones, within the household and with his death she loses the very centre of her system of support. It simply fades away. The Stroebes' theory exemplifies the idea of 'learned helplessness', describing how people come to think of themselves as helpless in the face of certain circumstances or demands, in this case of bereavement. In terms of adapting to death this approach encourages people to begin to evaluate their situation and take responsibility for themselves and come, if possible, to gain a new sense of identity through new activities and circles of friends.

## Aberbach and Charisma

Grief may also influence wider social life, as in David Aberbach's argument that early bereavement may influence adult personality in terms of the sociological notion of charisma and the charismatic personality (1989, 1996). His highly speculative theory supposes that the loss of a parent or cherished relative early in life can leave a person with a sense of abandonment that, in adult life, is compensated for by the support of many followers. He saw this pattern at work in some religious and political leaders who, in complex ways largely unknown even to themselves, seek followers and present themselves as worthy of being followed. While this is a complex topic open to serious criticism it cannot be ignored. Aberbach wonders, for example, just how the extensive and intense grief experienced by Hitler after the death of his mother, dying of cancer and whom he nursed during the final part of her illness, influenced his joining an anti-Semitic society soon after her death. Hitler's political rhetoric itself adopted the dramatic language of referring to the Jews as a cancer needing to be 'cut out if mother-Germany was to be saved' (Aberbach 1996: 28). A charismatic leader needs a following and there are contexts in which people need a leader. One such, as Aberbach also describes, was Germany after the First World War when a defeated people hardly possessed a family untouched by war-related death. 'In a society wracked with bereavement and the humiliation of defeat as Germany was after 1918, the need for well-being and unity can become especially pressing, and can point the way to dictatorship' (Aberbach 1996: 30). Here death becomes one integral element amidst several others and shows something of the complexity of human existence and how mortality and survival become explicitly powerful in the life of nations and, as it happened, the subsequent death of millions more in the drive for conquest. This extreme example is but one end of a spectrum of bereavement at the other end of which we have some like Tolstoy who lost his parents when young, with his brother and some other children dying later, all of which, in his case, made him realize the importance of 'belonging' (Gustavson 1986: 13).

## World Religions

I have explored Aberbach's idea in the case of Joseph Smith, the founder of Mormonism who was deeply affected by the death of his brother, Alvin. Joseph went on to found a religion fundamentally concerned with transcending death through temple rites for the dead grounded in extensive genealogical histories and with the hope of eternal glory for each extended family group (Davies 2000). Similar but less extensive examples can also be found in a number of Christian sectarian groups as also, arguably, for Islam whose founding prophet was soon orphaned, as were the founders of the Bahai movement (Davies 2002).

Whatever the origin of religions, it remains the case that they have been the prime channel for explaining and coping with death. Religious ritual has served to remove the dead while religious beliefs have underwritten their destiny, most especially through notions of morality, merit and judgement.

In the wider Indian tradition of Hinduism, Buddhism and Sikhism the notion of *karma* has been significant in describing the nature of moral acts and their outcome within the framework of transmigrating souls and reincarnation. The belief that individuals are responsible for their actions within a defined social context has been fundamental for what is thought to happen to the identity of people in their next life and until they are, ultimately, freed from the necessity of reincarnation. The caste system of India, one of the most extensive and enduring forms of social organization of humanity, affords a profound example of how a theory of death frames human forms of living in the light of past lives and in the hopes for the future. This social scheme can be interpreted in terms of social control in which religious ideas of merit and reincarnation are used to validate and justify the social position into which people are born. Some might see the fact that the priestly caste of Brahmins stands at the head of the hierarchy of worth in this scheme as questionable and, indeed, social reformers in India – not least Mahatma Gandhi – have sought to improve the lot of those reckoned to be at the base of the system of merit without them having to await their next incarnation.

Mention has already been made of the Jewish, Christian and Islamic view of resurrection as another way of dealing with the evaluation of moral life in relation to the divine. In all three the ultimate deity is operative in setting demands and making promises, often in the form of covenants, and in commanding allegiance and love from devotees. Within the many doctrines that interpret these divine–human relationships death plays a major part; indeed, it is inconceivable of viewing these religious traditions apart from their emphasis upon death and the destiny of believers. While this is obvious in the explicit supernaturalism of belief in individual resurrection, it also underlies that Jewish stream of thought which focuses on divine promises to an enduring people rather than on the private eternity of each of its members. Indeed, the history of the development of Jewish thought and of the Christian and Islamic traditions that emerged from it is a history of the rise of individual destiny amidst the destiny of a divinely chosen people, whether Jewish, Christian or Islamic.

## Identity and Religions

A sense of destiny is, perhaps, one of the strongest expressions of a sense of identity that is available to an individual. It is made even stronger when their community also reckons to possess a divine calling. At one level identity's power can be seen when two people fall in love with each other and express what has happened to them through the language of destiny. A very large number of popular songs root themselves in the language of a love that will last forever. In religious terms, too, there are those who speak of experiences that are not dissimilar in that they are in a love relationship with God and are aware of this in deeply personal terms. The popular love songs of the world at large become the devotional hymns and songs that now frame the believer's identity in a very special way.

Both historically and today, this highly charged personal awareness of a special link with the divine extending beyond death has been influential upon society. It comes to sharpest focus, perhaps, in martyrs. While it is not easy to understand one's own mind let alone anyone else's, it is especially hard for many, for whom life itself is the dominant concern, to see how people can wish to die for their religion. Much has been made in the opening years of the twenty-first century about Islam and 'Islamic Fundamentalists' engaging in what many non-Muslims see as acts of terrorism against what is perceived as western, morally corrupted, Christian capitalism. Some commentators refer to the rewards of paradise awaiting these 'martyrs' in terms that are, at best, ambivalent. It is as though the word 'fundamentalist' ensures a sense of unreality and lack of judgement over what is really the case in life, viz., a liberal and judiciously balanced preference for life at all costs and for a life lacking suffering. Some would like to interpret the acts of self-destruction and of terrorist-enforced death as some sort of pathological or primitive tribalism, and there may well be elements of that involved, but what cannot be ignored is the power of an identity gained from such self-sacrifice and in the life leading up to it.

The thought that death is but the entry to paradise with full honours must constitute one of religion's major achievements: far from fearing death it can now, openly, be embraced. Some early Christians went this way and so have representative brothers and sisters in subsequent generations, not least those who set out on missionary endeavours in the eighteenth and nineteenth centuries. So, too, in Hinduism, Sikhism and Buddhism, all of which can tell of those giving themselves in self-sacrifice for their belief or for the relief of those under oppression. For such the parting of death is but a full-blooded affirmation of human commitment to its ultimate purpose. Religion, above all ideological outlooks, can confer the strongest self-identity upon devotees, one that is so strong that death is but a means to its enhancement. Such strength can only be viewed as a prize and a peril: a prize for the saintly who use it not to harm but only to bless others and a peril for that kind of demonic person whose cast-iron, self-centred, will is now justified by divine fiat. For the majority, however, it is likely that life, death and whatever lies beyond is more a case of hope, optimism and faith pervaded to a greater or lesser extent by uncertainty, agnosticism and doubt.

One telling backdrop to bereavement interpreted as the loss of attachment is that of the Buddhist world-view with its ideological and practical warning of the problems inherent in the desire for attachment to 'things'. The apparently sweet desire to possess things that feed the powerful sense of 'self' and of who I am in this world turns bitter when we are deprived of them and, especially, when death removes them. The life of renunciation is not widely shared. Few foster that kind of 'mindfulness' which sees the world as it appears to us but does not bind itself to its illusion of permanence. Western individualized consumerism's need for constant support from commercialized sources of music and speech would become problematic if these were lost. Such dependency fuels many minor fires of 'loss' while the future alone will demonstrate how it may affect the great losses of life. Yet, everything remains a question of balance. The unrelated life is impossible for human society, just as for some Buddhists the ideal life of the celibate ascetic is only open to a few if wider society is to be reproduced and nurtured at all.

## Identity's Demise and Death

There is much in this Buddhist world-view that holds a strong attraction in western contexts of secularization, especially in times of religious change when the place of death within human identity changes. The Christian tradition moved from a human identity lodged in the success and destiny of a chosen people on earth, which it inherited from its Jewish origins, to a belief in a heavenly paradise. Today, however, much Jewish thought, and some Christian views too, witness a relative lack of emphasis on an afterlife, with a greater weight being placed on this world. Within Christianity, liberation theology in the later twentieth century gave pre-eminence to justice being accorded to the poor in this world rather than encourage dogged submission in the hope of heavenly rewards.

Perhaps the most interesting feature of the history of death in some major forms of contemporary Judaism and liberal Christianity lies in the demise of belief in an afterlife. It remains to be seen whether such liberal religion will maintain anything like an appeal to masses of people if its interest in an afterlife is abandoned. To this question we return in our final chapter.

## Adulthood–Childhood, Maturity and Death of Parents

Whatever views of the afterlife are held, the pain of grief remains real for many as they share the experience of 'parting's sweet sorrow'. In literary terms, on the occasion of their secretly pledged love, Shakespeare has Romeo and Juliet knowing that they must part before they are found together, and yet not wanting to be apart for a moment. Romeo's 'I would I were thy bird' is met by Juliet's,

> 'Sweet, so would I;
> Yet I should kill thee with much cherishing.
> Good night, good night. Parting is such sweet sorrow,
> That I shall say good night till it be morrow'
> (Romeo and Juliet, II.ii.).

Romeo leaves with words that form a kind of lover's blessing – the more poignant as part of the play haunted by echoes of biblical notions of love –

> 'Sleep dwell upon thine eyes, peace in thy breast.
> Would I were sleep and peace, so sweet to rest'.

Here, through the truth of a play, we move from the history of death on the large canvas of humanity to the autobiography of bereavement such as affects us all. One interesting aspect of bereavement is related to the increasing life-span of people in developed societies. From humanity's earliest days, mothers and family groups were accustomed to the death of many infants to the point, in some contexts, of not even according babies anything like a social identity until they were months, even years old. Not possessing a name, a baby would not receive a ritualized funeral if it died. This was true, to a degree, within European societies until well into the twentieth century, at least as far as newly born or stillborn babies were concerned.

Changing quality of life has affected relationships. With birth-control, smaller families, women as well as men pursuing jobs and careers, the very idea of having children has changed. Many plan pregnancy and ascribe a sense of identity to their baby long before it is born. Medical technology allows the foetus to be pictured within the womb; such scanning turns the foetus into a 'baby' and fosters its sense of identity long before birth. Two sides of foetal life in relation to adult identity thus emerge. Some see abortion as child-murder, others as the woman's right over her own body. Here ethics, identity, life and death starkly abut each other. Rapid developments in medicine and genetics have fostered the hope of otherwise childless people, just as they have addressed the inconvenience of unwanted pregnancy. This constitutes an important element in the history of death. It has, for example, magnified the loss of desired pregnancies, with the result that some still-births are treated as the death of someone who had, as it were, lived. Some Christian priests in England are known to have conducted baptism rites for children who never were alive in the world as such. Some hospitals allow for mothers or parents to be photographed with their stillborn or neonatally dead children to allow the woman a sense of identity as 'mother', something that would not have been the case in the past. Accordingly the 'death' of the child is, in a sense, socially marked and noted through some form of ritual whereas in the past it might even have been treated as unnamed 'biological waste'. It is as though the child is given a life, albeit for a moment, despite the fact of its death. Here the will and desire of the parents come to a kind of fruition despite the biological realities of the case.

Changing expectations in developed societies now assume that children will not die in infancy and, very largely, that parents will die before their children. This, itself, poses an intriguing aspect of modern life, viz., the identity of adult children. As generation succeeds generation the death of parents has allowed sons and daughters not only to gain an inheritance but to develop their own identity after the death of their parents. Individuals often come to see in themselves, in their very behaviour, aspects of their mother or father's posture or bearing so that, as one researcher expressed it, 'the body is the flesh of memory' (Young 2002). Such aspects of a son or daughter's sense of themselves as imaging or mirroring their deceased parent cannot fully develop as long as parents are alive and not until the child has attained the age of the parent as remembered in and through the mimicked behaviour. The death of parents marks a shift in responsibility and sense of self in the world; indeed, one might argue that parental death is integral to some fundamental aspect of adult maturity.

One consequence of contemporary life that might bear importantly upon this is the very early age of motherhood, perhaps especially for teenage girls who come to head single-parent families. If a girl gives birth, for example, when she is 16 years of age she will be only 76 when her son or daughter is 60. As likely as not the child will be 70 when the mother dies aged 86. At quite the other end of the scale there are those who, for reasons of career and because of medical advances, give birth aged 45. If these die at 86 their offspring, aged 41, are only just entering their fuller potential as adults. Just what consequences these age differences and demographic trends will yield await to be seen: certainly they should not be ignored in any survey of death in today's world. Carl Jung was one psychologist-philosopher who reflected on this issue and spoke of 'one sided people' – those whose maturity is delayed precisely because 'their parents are still alive' (1961: 120). Although generalization is problematic, two very different examples will illustrate this relationship between elderly parents and their offspring.

Georges Simenon (1903–89), author of over seventy of the Maigret detective novels spread over some forty years, offers one insight into bereavement. It seems as though his relationship with his mother, Henriete, was one in which she rejected his love; neither loved the other and knew it. The fondness often found between mother and son was absent. His biographer, Patrick Marnham, interpreted Simenon's immense literary productivity of some four to five novels a year as a response to his sense of worthlessness, suggesting that it was a means of overcoming his sense of rejection. 'When Henriete died his imaginary world died too . . . With her death the major emotional battle in his life was over' (Marnham 1992: 302). Whatever the psychological truth, Simenon stopped his novel writing within a year of her death, yet lived for another nineteen years.

Like Simenon, there are thousands of individuals, and the number is rapidly increasing in western societies, whose parents also live into old age. While this possesses numerous benefits in long-term relationships and potentially fruitful family networks, it may also provide a negative element in that the 'child', now perhaps near retirement, has never experienced personal grief in the loss of one or more parents. It is more likely that the 'loss' experienced in divorce or some other life crisis precedes the loss of parents.

Unlike Simenon, most will not have felt driven into creativity by negative parental relationships, but will, nevertheless, have had to live without that distinctive experience of becoming an 'adult orphan' with new responsibilities and sense of self. One public example in Great Britain might be found in the relationship between Queen Elizabeth II and the Prince of Wales. Since it is unlikely that Queen Elizabeth will ever abdicate the throne, it is only her death that will enable the Prince to become King. It is rare for an occupation to be so intimately associated with 'adult orphanhood', as we shall call it, but it exemplifies the principle that a 'child' may not become fully socially mature until its own parents die. In one sense this even happened to Queen Elizabeth, whose own mother – Queen Elizabeth, the Queen Mother – did not die until her daughter's fiftieth year on the throne.

## Moral-Somatic Links

Moving to a more theoretical argument, many of the cases and contexts considered in this chapter relate to what might be called the moral-somatic nature of life. This concept is important for understanding the nature of human identity and the way certain kinds of death impact upon it. While it is widely accepted that the mind influences the body, as the popular notion of psychosomatic issues demonstrates, it is less frequently appreciated that the social values and beliefs of a society also bear close links with the psychosomatic underpinning of life. It is to emphasize this link that I employ the idea of moral-somatic relationships. Human well-being is related to the fact that human beings are social creatures dependent upon the support and succour of a social group, whether of the family, clan, club, church or society at large. Grief takes its toll upon the bodily life of people not only because of the psychology of attachment discussed above but also because it is through partners, kin and friends, etc., that the moral nature of society is partly mediated. The very physical well-being of people is related to being in relationship with social values and to the sense that justice prevails. If and when a person considers that some deep injustice has been done to them they feel it as a body-state: people speak of 'feeling sick' or the like. This is especially the case when guardians of public morality are believed to have abused their position. While we develop this theme in the final chapter in relation to my 'theory of offending death' as applicable to various national tragedies, it is applicable here for cases of personal be-reavement which are deemed to be unfair. So, for example, while the death of an aged parent is often felt to be part of the natural scheme of things, with relatives experiencing grief, they do not regard the death as unnatural or unfair. The same cannot be said over the death of a young child or adult when severe illness or accident is deemed untimely and unfair. In some such cases it is God or the ultimate nature of life that is questioned. The wider religious and social expectations of people change over time as far as the 'fairness' of death is concerned but, cer-tainly, the social or moral explanations – or the lack of them – may take their toll of individual well-being.

## Spiritualism

When human well-being is disturbed by death, and a person finds it very hard to part with their relative, one option taken by some is to seek to contact the dead. Here Spiritualism becomes a viable option and can, in itself, either be part of a final process of bidding farewell or may become an ongoing means of develop-ing a sense of earthly identity through what is believed to be contact with the world-beyond. Spiritualism engages memory in a distinctive fashion, one that quite literally involves 'recalling' the dead by means of another human 'medium'. Spiritualism began within the single, Fox, family in Hydesville, New York in the late 1840s and, as the century advanced, developed into an identifiable practice with established congregations. While its belief that the individual's spirit passes at death from this world into the next closely resembles the practical belief of many reli-gious traditions, its distinctiveness derives from seeking to con-tact the dead and establish some sort of relationship between this life and those who have 'passed over' into the next. Main-stream Christianity generally objects to this element of contact, seeing in it reflections of forbidden images of witches conjuring up the dead. Nevertheless, ordinary Christians do sometimes attend Spiritualist séances in the hope of gaining a message from beyond the grave, a sense of comfort in knowing that their dead relatives are happy, and a degree of certainty of the afterlife. This tends to happen shortly after bereavement and very few continue to attend on a long-term basis. While major Christian traditions affirm life after death – doctrinally, ritually and pastorally – as an ultimate feature of human destiny, Spiritualism makes it proximate. To some grief-stricken relatives it is just such an immediacy of comfort that is sought, rather than a far-off goal framed by contemporary hopeful faith. Architecturally and geographically, Spiritualist churches often reflect the place of Spiritualism within society, certainly in Britain. In many suburbs and small towns the major denominations are present through the highly visible Anglican parish church and the relatively obvious buildings of the other denominations. The Spiritualist church, by contrast, is often a small building in a side or back street and reflects, in one sense, its partial relevance to people for a relatively short period after their bereavement.

The First World War provided Spiritualism with a newly extended arena of operation and attracted large numbers of grief-stricken relatives of fallen soldiers. One of its attractions lay both in the apparently experimental basis of mediums presenting evidence to those who sought succour in the séance and in Spiritualism's relatively open religious–secular boundary. Indeed the very doctrinal issue of salvation was ignored or placed very far behind the ongoingness of relationships between the living and the dead. In nineteenth-century USA the predominant Spiritualist emphasis lay upon universal salvation for all, rather than any narrower denominational restriction (Taves 1999: 195). The séance was, in a sense, a sacrament of eternal relations and an expression of the intuitive yet indeterminable nature of human love, memory and hope.

Within the history of death Spiritualism became to western societies what some aspects of Shamanism had been in many other societies. Shamanism is a form of ritual often involving trance assisted by various means, including drumming, dancing, drugs, as well as some form of prior apprenticeship or training. It sought to link the shaman with the realm of the spirits in order to gain some benefit for members of the shaman's society, often in terms of healing. In both Shamanism and Spiritualism we find an approach to death that reflects a theory of life grounded in a distinction between a soul and its human body, and in the relationship, balance or effect of each upon the other. And this was framed by the wider belief in this world and another, spiritual, world, and in the possibilities of benefit accruing from links between them.

For dedicated Spiritualists the sense of contact between the two worlds allowed each to help make sense of the other. Human life was better grasped by knowing that spirits existed after death, a belief that could be approached in ways that could foster the well-being of the living to a marked extent. Sir Oliver Lodge, for example, was a devotee of Spiritualism and in one of his writings tells of the compact made by a friend of his and her son, Christopher, before the young man went off to the 1914–18 war to meet his death (Lodge 1918). Both Christopher and his mother, from a much-involved Spiritualist family in South Wales, openly discussed the possibility of his being killed and of how he should seek to adjust himself in the afterlife by seeking 'dead' relatives and by coming to terms with his new environment. He should not, they agreed, immediately seek to comfort his mother by appearing in séances or the like but, when opportunity presented itself, they could establish some form of ongoing unity such as they had enjoyed at home. Published in 1918, *Christopher, A Study in Human Personality* stood as but one example of the millions of the war dead grieved by bereaved kin but, unlike most others, it depicts a context of dedicated Spiritualist belief in which attitudes to life and to death were framed in one spirit-focused vision of life.

## Departure

Whatever the belief about the soul, dead bodies have to be removed, a physical event that underlies the complex process of detachment. It is ironic that we often speak of the disposal of the body, since 'disposal' implies the getting rid of useless material whereas the corpse is often invested with considerable significance, as we will see more fully in chapter 8. Parting from the dead is both a psychological and social venture whose 'sweet sorrow' lies both in the new challenges presented and in the grief to be endured. The age of the dead and of the survivor, the nature of their social world and views of the afterlife all affect the bereaved, as will potent private longings and fears grounded in their resilience, health and power of hope.

# Chapter 3

# Removing the Dead

This chapter focuses on some of the dynamics of death rites involving ideas of the soul and human destiny on the one hand and varieties of funeral ritual on the other. A central concern lies both with the changing status of religion, especially Christianity, in the nineteenth and twentieth centuries, and with some of the conflicts that can emerge between individual belief and established religious practice. Special attention is paid to the emergence of modern cremation, especially in Great Britain, and to the consequential issue of the dignity of the dead in an increasingly secular world.

One common element within the history of death is the fact that actual corpses need removal; the dead demand some attention and treatment. This begins with the experience of death's strangeness, a phenomenon rooted in death's stillness which prompts beliefs to account for it and rites to cope with it. The dead are too still for the comfort of the living. Even when asleep people breathe, display eye movement and heartbeat. This makes the very inertness of death notable and marks these still-people as out of place amongst the living, sometimes regarded as ritually impure. Accordingly the dead are removed from the active realm of life.

Ways of physically removing the dead from the living have changed relatively little during the course of human history, with earth-burial and cremation continuing from earliest times to the present as the two basic forms of funeral. From the Old Stone Age period onwards, earlier even than the Chinchorro described in the previous chapter, evidence increases of bodies buried, sometimes in a foetal position, sometimes with grave goods and sometimes as cremated remains. Reflecting some formal treatment of the dead, these invite interpretation as ritual activity, with 'ritual', in turn, being assumed to involve some 'religion' including some afterlife belief. Just what an afterlife might have meant for those living some thirty thousand or more years ago it is impossible to say. Whether or not earliest humans had any notion of an afterlife, their formalized treatment of the dead does mark the symbolic power of bodies that had once been influential in the land of the living. Over time, burial and cremation have risen and fallen in popularity depending upon dominant religious beliefs and environmental possibilities. By contrast, mummification has decreased with time. The very small-scale contemporary option of cryogenics – the freezing of heads or bodies until some future date of medical cure and revivification – offers an echo of it but, we might assume, for quite different reasons. Rare, too, has been the custom of exposing the corpse for consumption by wild animals.

What has changed with time and varied greatly from society to society is the interpretation given to burial and cremation. To the burial or burning of bodies each society has brought its own distinctive beliefs expressing schemes of thought about the nature of life itself. In this chapter we consider two kinds of interpretation of death, one emphasizing theological and philosophical ideas and the other social scientific theories about the ritual of funerals. These are inextricably bound up with each other and need to be considered together.

Here 'religion' comes into its own as an identifiable field of human activity dealing with the meaning of life and death and helping provide the context for corpse removal. For corpses are never left around the living as so much waste but are removed in customary ways that follow a formal path of ritual convention. Ritual, as shared forms of patterned activity, focuses on significant social values and helps express how a people view the world and themselves. Although it is almost too obvious an observation, funeral ritual is particularly interesting because it deals with our very own nature. Much human activity is expressive and deals with the 'external' world of individuals but death rites are driven to consider the human being and its place in the nature of things. To remove the dead body from the realm of the living is something that is as close to instinctive as behaviour becomes, and so is the drive for an explanation of the reason for the death, ranging from witchcraft grounded in some malevolence on the part of a neighbourhood enemy to the very will of God. In many developed societies a medical or science-like explanation fills the explanatory gap.

The most common traditional explanation given for life, as for its absence in death, is that of some life-force, soul or spirit. This immaterial entity has been interpreted in a variety of ways but is regularly believed to come to the foetus in the womb to turn what is merely flesh and bone into a living person. The Greek idea of the immortal soul, the Hebrew notion of the life-giving breath or wind of God filling the person, the Indian sense of a reincarnating power bringing life to the body in the womb and leaving it through the cracked skull on the funeral pyre, and the Polynesian notion of an ancestral spirit coming to the pregnant mother on the waves of the sea: these and many other traditions account for life through some notion of spirit-power. The very sight of a dead body has been practical evidence enough to persuade many cultures of the life-giving spirit and its absence.

The wonder is that the remaining body has been so frequently treated with respect and not simply discarded as so much packaging, as nothing other than an empty shell. Here the sympathies, bonds of duty and memories of times past prompt an attitude of respect and the sense of dignity to which we return at the close of this chapter.

## Status and Destiny

One way of approaching the dead is to map where they are 'located' as deceased persons. At one end of the spectrum lie the largely forgotten dead, belonging to societies that acknowledge some shadow-land of the departed but who seek little or no contact with them. Though, through belief in ghosts, the living may still interact with the dead, they often wish to keep them at a distance. Where contact is fostered it is often in prescribed ways and at set times, as with ancestor cults and belief in an ancestral domain into which the dead pass. The ancestors may influence the living, by cursing them if basic social laws are broken or by blessing the obedient. Skulls, other remains or the names of the dead may be kept and honoured as they add some depth to a society, extending it beyond the living into the past and mirroring society's journey into the future through the off-spring of the living whose very fertility may be enhanced by ancestral benevolence.

Another band on this spectrum focuses on the life-force which, as the moral core of the once living person, now undergoes judgement after death as in ancient Zoroastrian traditions of Persia, as well as in Egyptian and Indian views. In the Indian outlook the judged life could undergo a series of non-earthly existences before reincarnating in this world, while for Middle Eastern thinkers the outcome involved a paradise or a hell with no reincarnating possibilities. Later, Judaism, Christianity and Islam set judgement after a single lifetime's experience and, after death, came either a resting in the grave until the day of resurrection and judgement or else a passing of the soul into the divine control for its final destination in heaven or hell.

One strong stream of Catholic thought also favoured belief in a period of purgation during which the sinful soul could be prepared for its final consummation in the ultimate vision of God. Though for much of the sixteenth to nineteenth centuries Protestant theology was very like Catholicism in believing in an immortal soul, the twentieth century witnessed an increased formal Protestant emphasis upon the resurrection of the body and not upon the soul. These aspects of destiny all have funeral rites expressing their prime views and making the outcome possible. Catholics came to speak much of the journey of the Christian soul and its welcome into the world beyond, while Protestant theologians dwelt upon the resting in peace until the final time of resurrection. Many lay-Protestants, however, continue to think in terms of souls. Still others, including some in the Orthodox tradition, have favoured an emphasis upon the way God holds all people, as it were, in the divine mind and, in that sense, maintains them in 'being' until such time as they become newly resurrected and are able to assume in a new way their proper identity. Church liturgies of death express these variations in their prayers and hymns, though we cannot explore them here (cf. Sheppy 2003).

## Ritual Change

What we can do, however, is sketch how some anthropologists have accounted for the way ritual helps transform the identity of the dead in the minds of the living as the corpse is removed. Here two contributions are particularly important, viz., those of Arnold van Gennep and Robert Hertz.

Van Gennep inaugurated the idea of rites of passage in a book published in 1906. He saw death rites, along with many other rituals that change a person's status, as a threefold scheme of separation from the old status, a period of transition – often involving intensive learning of new expectations – and an incorporation into the new status. He expressed surprise that while one might expect funerals to emphasize the element of separation, they actually tended, by contrast, to emphasize transition. As for mourning, he regarded it as a transitional period for survivors (1960: 146–7). Van Gennep did not claim 'an absolute universality or an absolute necessity for the pattern of rites of passage' (1960: 161). Where they do occur he saw them as regenerating social processes that, otherwise, have their energy exhausted (1960: 182). In this sense, rites of initiation, for example, 'take the form of rites of death and rebirth', with death and rebirth becoming analogies of and metaphors for changes experienced during one's lifetime (1960: 182).

Van Gennep's contemporary, Robert Hertz, focused even more specifically on death rites, showing how some South East Asian pre-literate societies took a twofold form, firstly moving the corpse from the realm of the living and, secondly, installing the 'deceased' in the realm of the ancestors (Hertz 1960 [1907]). This movement of the dead from one world to another could be symbolized by describing the human remains as in a 'wet' or 'dry' stage. First the 'wet' corpse would decay and, as it did so, its ties with its past life, its status, duties and obligations would be reduced. At the same time the relatives would grieve and undergo, within themselves, some changes of attitude towards the dead. In other words, grief paralleled decay. During this period the corpse might be buried or stored and then, decay completed, the 'dry' bones would be exhumed and become the symbolic basis for the new identity awaiting the deceased as an ancestor: new rites would make it so. Hertz saw with particular clarity that human society becomes, in a sense, embodied in living persons. Throughout life we take upon ourselves and absorb into ourselves the values and the very nature of our society. It is as though society is 'within' us. At death this needs teasing out or reversing as we are removed from ordinary society to become a member of the other-world.

In traditional Indian cremation, as also with Sikhs and Buddhists, the burning of the dead is followed by the collection of ashes for placing in rivers which are deemed sacred. Meanwhile the life-force passes from the body in the process of its ongoing reincarnation before final release into the ultimate nature of things. Rites are performed at different periods after cremation to aid the journey of the soul and also to bring the survivors into a new sense of relationship with the departed 'person'.

Traditional Jewish funerals at the time of Jesus also followed double burial, with the dry bones being collected and placed in special containers – ossuaries – which remained in tombs. Although many Christians often talk about early Jewish thought as not involving any extensive ideas of life after death, such views did exist, and subsequently developed into firm beliefs in resurrection. Not only so, but some Jews also held a belief in a soul or life-force that animated the body during life, that remained near the corpse during the period after death and demanded due deference from the living. Even the anointing of 'dead' bodies can be interpreted as a means of helping to calm the 'dead' individual as, through death, he or she atones for his or her sins. Death itself came to be regarded as a means by which a person might atone for the sins committed during life, as discussed in chapter 1.

## Resurrection

Christianity also took the idea of the resurrection of Jesus as something that would, in the fullness of time, also happen to the rest of humanity. This belief intersected with the idea of divine judgement in ways that were not always in perfect harmony. Was human destiny decided by belief in Jesus whose death saved believers from judgement, ultimate death and hell, or would believers also have to face a judgement despite their belief? Here theological differences sometimes emerged. Whichever was the case, the idea of heaven as an ultimate destiny of those granted salvation became prominent, especially in the medieval period, when it was set against vivid portrayals of hell as a place of torment as chapter 5 shows. Christianity favoured the burial of the dead, seeing it as mirroring the 'burial' of Christ, even though his was a tomb burial and not an inhumation as practised by northern Europeans. Such customs came to be normative and were 'exported' in the great missionary period of the eighteenth and nineteenth centuries as these churches taught their own cultural forms in many a context, whether appropriate or not.

Burial took place with the dead facing east or towards Jerusalem, symbolically awaiting Christ's return. Even though Christians might disturb the bones of the dead and place them in parish ossuaries or crypts, as was customary amongst the Greek Orthodox, this process has to be interpreted with care. In one sense the logic of double funeral rites was unusual: Christians buried the dead in sure and certain hope of the resurrection but it was for God to resurrect them on the last day and, in that way, provide the future identity for the deceased. In Hertz's scheme of things we could say that humans completed the first 'burial' and removal of identity from the land of the living, with God completing the second stage by conferring an eternal status on the deceased. Other forms of interpretation are also possible; so, for example, in popular forms of Greek Orthodoxy when the dead were exhumed after several years it was a cause for concern if they had not decayed. Indeed, lack of decay indicated that the dead had been either a saint or a great sinner: life circumstances were used to decide which it was. If a sinner, the body would usually be reburied with special prayers asking for a decay to occur so that the soul might find its peace with God. Saints, by contrast, might be kept as relics and used as part of popular devotion: body-parts carry their own symbolic message across the ages.

Such devotional responses in relation to the dead have been very extensive in human history, but times change. While it is not always easy to grasp the nature of one's own day and age, it is worth trying to understand how the later twentieth and early twenty-first centuries involve shifts in human values and perspectives that may be quite revolutionary. Here death serves as a window into change.

Although difficult to generalize on afterlife beliefs, it is important to have some sense of differences present in today's world. In terms of religious belief and practice, for example, some cope with the major differences existing between 'secular' western Europe on the one hand and the 'religious' USA and many other parts of South America and Africa on the other, by describing Europe as an 'exceptional case'. They see high levels of religious attendance and acknowledgement of belief in Christianity, Islam, Hinduism and Buddhism as rooted in a different form of social life than that of secular Europe. Some recent shifts in the way intellectuals ponder matters of 'truth' have made this situation more problematic, as some discussions on postmodernity accept that groups can believe what they like without criticism. This view does an injustice to human thought and to ways of viewing the world that have emerged through long experience in what have become major scientific, philosophical and sociological disciplines. There is, it seems to me, a cumulative wisdom that develops in and through critical thought that is abandoned only at one's peril. But, it seems to me, times are changing and parts of Europe are leading that change rather than constituting 'an exceptional case'. Here I risk the criticism of following a kind of imperialist and colonialist view in respect of secularization in which European 'civilization' leads the world, not to mention a kind of evolutionary argument over religion in which religious 'stages' of human history pass over into 'scientific' stages. Those criticisms are worth risking in order to follow one social scientific view of human life and of changes within societies. I do this because I think that death, and human views of death, offer a distinctively instructive window into human self-reflection and self-understanding.

## Changing Times

Death rites relate very largely to established notions of an afterlife and for most of its history humanity has believed in some kind of afterlife that is related to social rules. Life in this world is related to the life that will be led in the next. This linkage has, of course, been influential on the thinking of critics of religion who see the promise of heaven and paradise or the threat of hell as a means of controlling human life based upon false beliefs.

By contrast, we might draw attention to what has become a shift into a this-worldliness in Europe through the second half of the twentieth century. Much could be said about the philosophical roots of agnosticism or atheism grounded in the Enlightenment, as also on the rise of science as a major source of knowledge; indeed, much could also be added on the development of liberal theology within major religions, especially in Protestant traditions, in the nineteenth and twentieth centuries. Similarly, the rise and fall of Communist ideologies have made their mark. But, all this apart, it is the general and popular drift from a religiously influenced view of the world to one in which religion is marginal or ignored that is of interest here. And it is in and through the way people deal with death that I see that drift taking place. Here, England and, for example, Australia are in the lead.

## Default Religion

Our searchlight upon funerals, death and destiny falls upon the churches on the one hand and individuals, the family and friends of the dead on the other. European Christian churches, especially major Protestant churches, have decreased their emphasis upon the afterlife to a considerable degree; hell is seldom mentioned and is, in fact, practically an ignored topic, while heaven has, if anything, become an optimistic way of speaking about the enduring nature of human relationships. Heaven is more therapeutic than theological. At the same time the kin and friends of the dead are increasingly taking part in funeral rites. The choice of non-biblical readings from poems or literature often replaces or complements scriptural material and is used to express the personal relationship with the deceased or to highlight some aspect of the life and experience of the one who has died. It is the personal and individual note that is struck. Though religious venues are often chosen, and religious leaders regularly conduct proceedings, it is far from certain that this is because of the key religious doctrines they represent. It is likely that they bring a cultural frame of seriousness to moments of emotional complexity. More than that, circumstances of death and funerals are such that in contemporary societies there is what might be called a cultural 'default position': in other words, if no specific decision is taken to the contrary then one path will be followed. The historical background of Christianity in Europe, and much the same could be said for other major religions in the countries of their historical dominance, makes it natural and 'normal' for clergy to conduct funerals. This is the easier option for people, even those with little or no active religious belief or commitment.

Funeral directors are of particular importance in the rites of death and they tend to be particularly conservative in matters of customary behaviour. They tend to encourage and certainly not to discourage established ways of doing things, not least because it is easier to ensure a satisfactory performance. They may have particular priests or ministers with whom they work well. Against that weight of expectation bereaved people would need a very special reason and relatively strong motivation to choose quite a different pattern for a funeral. To elect not to have a religious functionary or venue raises many questions about what to do and how to do it, issues that may be hard to resolve over the short and intense period of an immediate bereavement. It is much easier to adopt the default position and then to request personal readings or personal music as markers of individuality set within the traditional framework.

Many clergy, for their part, are happy to engage with people in these requests. They do so for many reasons. In part it is an expression of pastoral care and a means of discovering family dynamics with the potential for future contact. It is also a means of being accepted by people who may not be actively involved with churches. The alternative would be to try to impose a traditional form against the will of the bereaved, and the mood of society would hardly make that feasible. There is, also, for some churches, a very real financial incentive, with the fees from conducting funerals making a significant contribution to church income. All in all, a collaboration between priest and the bereaved family and friends can yield a highly satisfactory rite in which elements from the 'great tradition' of Christianity combine with local and personal items reflecting the desire of family and friends to mark the individuality of this particular dead person.

This emphasis upon the individual and the relationships with the living marks a change from traditional Christian rites which, even until the closing decades of the twentieth century in Britain, tended to treat the dead as one of the general class of God's 'sons and daughters' or of those who were becoming part of the heavenly kingdom or of the communion of saints. References to our 'dearly departed brother' or 'sister' saw the deceased as a Christian in general and not a named family member or as a friend of named individuals in particular. Many clergy were trained in the early and middle parts of the twentieth century to think in this way about the dead and were not encouraged to engage in eulogies on the virtues of the deceased nor to dwell upon their idiosyncrasies. Much of that has now changed and marks, within the history of death, a shift to the importance of the individuality of each person – as individual in death as in life.

To move from this combined position of tradition and customized treatment of the dead to one in which the traditional theological element falls away, leaving only the customized form, might not be at all difficult. Many people may think that one 'must have a priest' for a funeral, which is not the case, and once that fact becomes widely known and acted upon by funeral directors a change of the default position might emerge relatively quickly. For some funeral directors this would be an advantage because they might decide to serve as officiants at services, thereby intensifying their relationship with the deceased and building into their relationship an after-care service for the bereaved, something which many priests find it difficult or impossible to do for reasons of time or because the people are simply not church-involved. Already a few funeral directors in England are engaging their own officiants and bereavement counsellors.

## From Respect to Dignity

Central both to custom and innovation is the idea of the 'dignity' of the dead, a word that is increasingly influential. We have already seen how death rites mark the changing status of the dead. This does not mean that the position the dead held during their life is ignored but that it is acknowledged as death now takes the individual away. Life relationships involve respect as part of the mutual obligations people owe each other, and these elements of respect and obligation also progress through funeral rites. To speak of the dignity of the dead is to mark the respect they were paid during life and to indicate that certain obligations still remain. Dignity is the form taken by respectful duty when the subject is dead. But 'dignity' includes yet another feature; it is the very fact that human bodies bear life itself. 'Life' is not as easy to define as may at first appear; indeed, the development of medical science and technology has made it more complex than it was before, and yet it is the basic feature of human, as of other forms of existence. Though life-support machines may perpetuate the existence of human bodies, for the great mass of people the difference between life and death is stark and obvious. The value that has been brought to bear upon 'life' as the human species has taken ever more complex forms of social and cultural life upon itself is quite marked. The United Nations' Charter for Human Rights is but one example of the 'value of life' and of the ever-increasing sense of the 'quality of life' that developed societies see as imperative for fostering through politics and every other means possible. The very notion that 'life is cheap' in particular contexts has become anathema to those charged with political leadership, let alone religious leaders for whom the 'value of the individual before God' has become a charter for many forms of welfare activity.

The main enemy of the value of life at the beginning of the twenty-first century is the value of money in the hands of those deemed to be criminal and who 'use people' as the means of their own enrichment. The modern form of slavery described as 'trafficking in people' – with monetary extortion triggering illegal immigration for work or for sexual prostitution – is one sign of the moral complexity of contemporary life. It is precisely in such contexts that life becomes 'cheap' and the death of many a mere incident in the process of international criminality. Similarly with terrorism, and the political wars of numerous societies.

In economically successful parts of developed societies of Europe, America and Australasia life has become increasingly viewed as precious, with attitudes that extend to the natural environment as the matrix for human survival and flourishing. Against that kind of transformed view of life the dignity of the dead takes on additional significance as a this-worldly concern. Many speak of the dignity of the dead precisely because of the importance of life in a world of increasing options for self-development.

## Death-Style and Belief

Contemporary life, especially for those in successful parts of developed societies, has become increasingly grounded in personal choice over lifestyle, accentuated and facilitated by consumerism. Within such market-economies it is possible to speak not only of lifestyle but also of death-style. One of the most distinctive features of these particular twenty-first-century consumers is that a significant number in developed societies no longer believe in a life after death. Here the difference between the USA and many western European countries is considerable. Levels of general religious practice and belief in the USA are higher than in most European countries, and this extends to ideas of the afterlife.

Although Communism is easily forgotten after its rapid decline in the USSR and other European countries in the closing decades of the twentieth century, it was, in its day, influential in creating rituals to cover many aspects of life, from the first day at school to actually becoming a member of the working class. Death was no exception; forms of funeral rites were actively constructed for the party faithful and were, obviously, not based on religious tenets. In Russia, for example, cremation was strongly encouraged, partly as a means of weaning Orthodox Christians away from their traditional funeral liturgies. Cremation in many other European societies, especially in the northern countries with a Protestant cultural heritage, allowed new rites to emerge that drew people away from the sole influence of the churches. In chapter 8 we will return to these issues in terms of this-worldly attitude towards human destiny, not least in relation to growing ecological concerns.

## Cremated Remains

Crucial to changes in belief over the afterlife and to rites that express those changes is modern cremation. Cremation made a new appearance in Europe only from the 1860s when numerous groups of freethinkers began discussing it as a possible way of dealing with the dead. Most large cities witnessed debates or the emergence of cremationist interest groups. There were two major reasons behind these debates; sometimes they overlapped and sometimes were identifiable as distinct motives. One concerned medical and scientific concerns with the overfull urban cemeteries that followed the industrial revolution and the marked growth in size of many conurbations. Rotting corpses buried too near the surface or crypts of churches in which bodies could be smelt came to be identified with disease and were a source of distaste. Movements for sanitary reform and modern developments in town planning pressed for the legalization of cremation and for the building of appropriate facilities. By and large this moved into acceptance in the period 1889–1910 so that as the twentieth century got under way cremation was in place even though it was a minority practice. The two major world wars, in which many men died and were buried or lost away from home, shook many countries free from established notions of every parishioner safely 'asleep' in a local cemetery and opened the possibility for cremation to be an option in a way that might well not have occurred but for the wars. By the mid-1960s in England cremation overtook burial as the dominant form of funeral and by the beginning of the twenty-first century some 70 per cent of the British dead were cremated.

This was not the case, however, in European countries with a Catholic cultural history and this is where the second major reason for cremation pressure groups makes its presence felt. In Italy in the nineteenth century, groups pressing for cremation tended to include many influential Freemasons who were also freethinkers and not devoted members of the Catholic Church. Indeed, Catholic leaders saw cremation as an expression of secularism and of an anti-Christian attitude. In other words, cremation became an arena of competition over the meaning of human life and its destiny. For such freethinking people to join together and build a cremation 'temple' that was, very specifically, not a Catholic church starkly made the point. It took nearly a century, until the mid-1960s, for Catholic leaders to accept cremation as a valid form of funeral as long as it was not intended as an anti-Christian act. In most northern European countries Freemasons were not anti-Christian and any involvement of theirs with cremation did not attract this negative response.

Nevertheless, once cremation became established, other factors of social change brought a decrease in belief both in a traditional Christian form of afterlife and in seeing churches as the only acceptable agents to deal with the dead. In fact the Christian denominations were, conceptually, very slow to adapt to cremation in that they used old forms of burial rites as the means of conducting cremation with, for example, a continued symbolic sense of burial and resurrection and a virtual lack of mention of cremation as such. Special church rites, acknowledging these changes, did not, essentially, emerge until the 1980s and, by then, individuals had, slowly but steadily, begun to take matters into their own hands. When remains had been deposited in columbaria, been scattered or buried they had, essentially, been set within the public domain and placed there either by clergy or officers of crematoria; a newly emerging custom of taking remains away from the crematorium marked a shift from this public to a private domain.

Certainly, this development expressed a new form of relationship between the individual and society at large or between a family and society at large. It marked one form of secularization in that ecclesiastical control no longer extended over the remains of the dead as it had done when bodies were buried in churchyards or cemeteries after appropriate religious rites. Within that private realm a host of new factors came into play; some expressed the personal and psychological dynamics of the bereaved, others reflected aspects of family and domestic politics. Some of these themes will be addressed again in chapter 6 in the context of the changing nature of hope and its impact upon people.

Positively, this allowed individuals to express grief in distinctively personal ways and also allowed them to memorialize the dead in terms of the deceased's personality and interest. Here a marked contrast can be drawn between traditional Christian theology and liturgy of death and the new individualized mode of secularity, at least as far as the identity of the dead, and of the living in relation to the dead, was concerned.

Traditional Christianity spoke of a fulfilment of individual identity that lay in eternity, as we explain more fully in chapter 6. The theology of the resurrection and the words and form of Christian funeral liturgy fully supported this view. The individualized mode of private placing of remains, by contrast, generally set the identity of the dead within their former biography, with remains located in places of special personal significance. In this the living constructed their memory of the dead in terms of their known and experienced past, in terms of active memory. This complex process of memory and grief and the ongoing life of the bereaved was, to a degree, made even more complex if ecclesiastical funeral rites conflicted with the personal beliefs and values of the dead and the bereaved.

Once removed from the public domain of clear expectation of what happens to the remains of the dead, the choice of their destination can become problematic. Family members may disagree over whether to divide the remains or leave them as a single entity; they may also wish to place them in different places. Similarly, it can be problematic if the remains are placed in the garden of a private house which is subsequently sold. Individuals can also change their minds over time, or encounter emotions they did not anticipate. One example can be conveniently drawn from the biography of Georges Simenon whose Inspector Maigret has entranced millions of detective story addicts. After Simenon's daughter Marie-Jo's suicidal death he had her cremated remains scattered under an impressive cedar tree at their garden in Lausanne. Not only did his, then, wife describe this decision as 'obnoxious', because she saw it as depriving her of a grave that could be visited, but it also resulted in Simenon no longer going into that garden which, hitherto, had been much loved (Marnham 1992: 316–9). In this case a place of memory had become one of bad memories and of complexities of relationships that were, if anything, aggravated by a private decision to move the dead from the more neutral territory of the public cemetery or graveyard.

## Space, Cryogenics and Computers

Consumerist death-style has, as might be expected, only burgeoned with a market economy in which entrepreneurs set their creativity to offer new forms of death service for the removal of the dead. This has, for example, witnessed companies prepared to send cremated remains into outer space, to freeze bodies that have died through untreatable illness, and to set up memorial websites. Each of these provides an example of human adaptation in the quest for death-conquest.

To have one's cremated remains sent into orbit around the earth or into outer space is to share in the scientific and technological endeavours that, during the second half of the twentieth century, enshrined a wider sense of human conquest and hope for the future. It is likely that those very few individuals able to afford such post-mortem provision have desires that bring a sense of added hope to their grasp of the meaning of life. Perhaps this cluster includes the symbolic load previously carried by 'the heavens' as a place of divine dwelling.

Similarly with freezing the dead. This technology of cryogenics is also framed by a scientific capacity pervaded by a human hope for the future. There is tremendous belief inherent in the idea that someone who has just died of a terminal illness can be taken and frozen, or indeed have only their head frozen, and kept until such time as medical science is able to cure the illness and either revive the corpse or revive the head and provide it with some kind of cloned body. Once more, this is a costly venture and shows how money comes to the aid of a potential conquest of death. The ethical and commonsense ideas entailed by cryogenics seem to pass relatively untouched, even though the vision of being revived in a future world devoid of one's current environment and networks of family and friends is one that not all would value.

# Chapter 4

# Ecology, Death and Hope

By discussing some of the contexts within which death and corpses assume significance, including prison, the poor-house, death at home, in hospices and as soldiers, this chapter opens up the question of the values and beliefs associated with human bodies. It assumes that the history of death involves a history of the value of a human life. This then provides the basis for a major consideration of ecology and the way relatively new ideas of the world and our place in it may affect attitudes to death, disposal and destiny and to the changing manifestation of human hope. This is an important part of this book because it raises the possibility that the modern world is on a cusp of customary change as far as death is concerned. In one sense it is a shift from a religious to a 'spiritual' engagement with death.

## Criminals, Heretics, Bodies and Belief

Historically speaking, those judged to have betrayed the monarch or state had not only been tortured but executed, drawn, quartered and disembowelled. In other words, their bodies were desecrated as much as possible. They suffered the greatest indignity precisely because they were regarded as having committed the highest of crimes against society or monarch as its symbolic head. In a similar way the torture and burning of heretics or those convicted of witchcraft in medieval Europe and elsewhere expressed the belief that they had served the devil against God as represented by the dominant church of the day. To be burnt at the stake was in itself the final symbol of degradation, of removing from society those deemed to pollute it. This reinforced the biblical images of fire as the medium of torment of the wicked after death, as reinforced centuries later by the Nazi use of cremation to destroy the bodies of the Jews and others killed in what was regarded as the 'final solution' in purifying the forthcoming and new 'empire' – the third Reich – that would replace the earlier Holy Roman Empire.

Death is regularly symbolic of values espoused by a society as another example shows, one associated with changes in England's poor law in the 1830s which allowed for the bodies of those who died in poverty and in the local workhouse to be taken to medical schools for dissection (Richardson 1987). Hitherto bodies for dissection had come only from executed criminals so, in a practical sense, the poor were now, to all intents and purposes, criminalized. To some minds dissection was not far from the executioner's butchery. This was one reason why the desire for a proper funeral became an intensely strong wish amongst the working classes of the ongoing nineteenth century and raises the issue of the dignity of the dead. If dignity for the dead is an extension of the respect they held in life, as the previous chapter suggested, then this case of the criminalized poor shows just how, in life, they were accorded but little status, so that one could hardly expect it to suddenly appear at their death. But, for individuals themselves, a sense of personal respect did extend into the hope for dignity in death: and this very notion of self-respect was one that held a high place amongst some of the working classes of Britain over centuries, and into the present. Precisely because of that, we would expect the notion of dignity to appear once people addressed themselves to the question of death, and this is just what happened through the rise of mutual associations and burial societies in Victorian Britain whose very existence served to arrange the funerals of the poor.

## Dying at Home

To die at home had long been an ideal in many societies and, until the middle of the twentieth century, most people did so, with their bodies being retained there until their funeral. Families were often assisted by the traditional services of local people who helped prepare dead bodies. During the nineteenth century funeral directors became increasingly evident as service providers for the bereaved. To die at home ensured that death was a local and relatively ordinary event, one integrated within the family and neighbourhood community. Having the body in the house enabled family members to see the dead, talk to them and generally reflect on life. Neighbours and friends, too, could call and share sympathies as they talked about the deceased and reminisced about the past, all as part of the changing times that a death brings about.

In the post-war period of relative poverty this continued to make good sense but changes soon occurred. In Great Britain the welfare state was created and, with it, a rise in the standard of living involving such things as domestic central heating which some saw as a problem in keeping the dead at home during the winter, and even the removal of separate 'parlours' in many working-class homes to make larger 'living-rooms' with the resulting loss of any distinctive place for extremely formal events such as the placing of a coffin. It may even have been the case that with smaller numbers of family members living in a house it was less easy for the few individuals present to bear the sense of grief of being in the house on their own with the dead. However, improved medical services soon witnessed increasing numbers of people being hospitalized and dying in hospital while, at the same time, the profession of funeral director expanded its scope through the provision of funeral 'parlours' or funeral homes. The dead could now be collected from hospital, prepared at a funeral director's premises and be kept there until the funeral, with ample provision being made for the family to visit the deceased. Even religious services could be held at the chapels associated with many such new provisions. The older custom of a brief service in the house prior to the church service or the service at the cemetery or crematorium was now relocated. From the 1950s and 60s, crematoria also increased in number and practically always included chapels or halls in which funeral services could be held. In one sense they replaced ordinary chapels and churches and aided the relocation of death as far as traditional locations were concerned. Even though crematorium chapels might be specially adapted chapels that had already existed in older cemeteries, or were built to be like those, their very location, away from the township sites of parish churches and chapels, enabled a degree of difference to emerge in some people's minds. Each of these shifts in funeral context involved a degree of re-evaluation of the significance of a life. To move the dead from the home to a funeral home implicitly reduced family ties with the corpse, just as the use of increased services from undertakers involved acceptance of higher levels of service provision in an increasingly consumerist society. Similarly, to die in hospital after a medically controlled illness and a closely supervised death could be viewed as a form of professional control of death.

## Hospice

Not all were happy with what they saw as this medicalization of death. The controlling figures of doctors in hospitalizing the seriously ill and dying was regarded by some as a form of depersonalization and a kind of marginalizing of the family, let alone the unfortunate locating of the dead in unfamiliar territory. One response to this was the rise of the hospice movement which transformed the hospital ethos into patient- and family-focused contexts in which the terminally ill could be welcomed to live out their final weeks and days in as full and self-aware a way as possible. Improved medical capabilities to control pain, especially for those terminally ill with various cancers, also became foundational to hospice life.

Special places of this kind have been known for centuries, especially in relation to religious traditions of charity and preparing the dead for the world to come, but, especially in the mid- and later twentieth century, they also began to place emphasis upon the broad notion of 'spirituality' and also 'holistic' therapy. The very breadth of the notion of spirituality as a description of the importance of the awareness of the quality of a depth within life and existence matches the therapeutic intent of holism as a desire to view each individual not as a set of body-parts or discrete illnesses but as a whole person set within a network of wider relationships. This is a good example of the way in which the history of death is related to changing views of the 'person'. Hospices were and are, increasingly, often strongly supported by volunteers who appreciate these perspectives and who often speak of the hospice's supportive capacity, ensuring that the dying are not marginalized to, as it were, a hospital side-ward or room, but are the main focus of the life and work of each hospice. Some critics, however, take the view that hospices remove the dying from their home and, thereby, marginalize the dying and death to an even greater extent. Here much depends upon one's point of view and individual experience.

While many hospices possess a strong Christian motivation and include many active believers amongst their personnel, staff and supporters believe that their general goal is not to press beliefs upon anyone but to encourage each person to work out their own thoughts and needs as they prepare to die. In and through the hospice movement we witness the positive value placed upon dying as a kind of conclusion to life. It is affirmative of death in terms of the individual's life story and, as far as possible, its completion, resolution and consummation. In that sense the hospice outlook takes seriously the popular phrase of 'unfinished business' and would be content to be seen as providing a context and an atmosphere in which a dying person has the opportunity to engage with such business and do what he or she wishes to do in respect of it.

## Symbolic Bodies

In these hospice-related values the dying person is viewed much as those in full health would be, as individuals set in relationships with others and as worthy of care and attention as they seek to fulfil their lives. Life-values are maintained into the period of dying. This contradicts one widely found outlook which pretends that death does not exist or, certainly, will not befall any specific individual. People may talk about death in general but not about their own death, an issue to which we return in chapter 7 in an observation of Albert Schweitzer from the early twentieth century. Here we take one example from British television in 2003 which focused on the contrast between fictional and real corpses. The twenty-first century began with increasing media attention being given to dead bodies as they appear in detective or war films – a developing genre of risk-films that hint at the hazards surrounding contemporary life. Seldom does any British murder-hunt forget to include at least one visit to the morgue where a post-mortem is under way. The pathologist and detective look down upon the mangled victim who appears on screen only as a covered corpse or with selected limbs exposed. Though cosmetics have done their best, the 'dead' actor seldom appears so. Several other kinds of programme have serialized the lives of funeral directors, real or fictive. Once again, the 'corpse' is regularly invisible. This kind of familiarity symbolizes to a great degree the nature of death in contemporary Britain; everyone knows that it is there but it is largely invisible. Death may, by some, be feared – it is an obvious life 'risk' – but it somehow becomes domesticated through the media. If death was 'medicalized' in the mid- to late twentieth century, at the turn of the new millennium it became increasingly 'media-ized'. It is safe when viewed in comfort.

One event, however, disturbed this calm in 2002–3. Dr Peter von Hagens, a German pathologist, had perfected a process of what he called plastinization, enabling the replacement of body fluids with a plastic solution that made it possible for excellent dissections to be performed and maintained as exhibits. This individual mounted just such an exhibition that was taken on tour and, in London for example, attracted thousands of visitors along with much media attention. But this was nothing compared with his mounting a public event in which he performed a dissection of a human corpse. Tickets were sold and an audience gathered, as also did television cameras. Wearing a distinctive trilby hat von Hagens performed the act. The criticism levelled against him was considerable; many emphasized the 'performance' element and the hat, indicating that the dignity of the dead was impugned and voicing the opinion that such a thing should not occur in public. The facts that people paid for the privilege of being there and that the media turned up to film it reflect something of an interest in death and a concern to see what is normally forbidden. Whatever voyeuristic thrill may have been involved in this, the case pinpoints the complex duplicity over death in contemporary society. Von Hagens' exhibition reflected in a significant fashion the scientific concern with the human body and its health and that is, partly, reflected by many Britons who show real interest in their fitness. Nevertheless, a significant portion of the population is overweight and apparently unconcerned about their state of health.

In all the preceding cases the human body and its 'person' were highly charged with significance and show how the symbolic power of living and dead bodies brings to the history of death the history of changing social values. The final two cases highlight such values in the context of twentieth-century USA, one focused on the cosmetic treatment of the corpse and the other on the death of soldiers.

Jessica Mitford's highly popular book *The American Way of Death* described how funeral directors prepared bodies through intense cosmetic work before holding party-like funerals for them in funeral homes (1963). This was a strong critique of commercialization of the death 'industry'. Certainly, many parts of the USA do prepare the dead so that they look much as they did in life and this cosmetic realism can be read as a form of the denial of death, as can its corresponding practice of burying the dead in substantial caskets within brick or concrete-lined graves. Part of the cosmetic process usually involves embalming which, to the bereaved, may give the sense of very long-term preservation of the corpse even though the real effect is often short lived. Embalming carries with it some hint of the ancient Egyptian practice that was long lasting but which was also quite different in that it did not end by simply replacing the blood as modern embalming largely does, but also detached the entire internal organs and brain. In this area of human life detail is often ignored and only some preferred sense of benefit is accepted. Certainly this cosmetic–casket–concrete complex seeks to express preservation of the dead even though, in practice, it really leads to the inevitable corruption of the body within its casket rather than in contact with the earth. This approach could be read as an expression of the value of the American individual whose identity is preserved and maintained.

Mitford's account fits into an extensive literature on the acceptance or denial of death in the USA to which we return in chapter 7 when discussing the fear of death. Here I draw attention to quite a different view of death in America that adds a distinctive dimension to it and specifically concerns the death of soldiers in the service of the USA; it is of particular interest in the light of the twin towers terrorist attack of September 2001 and in the subsequent political and military response in the Iraq war. Carolyn Marvin and David Ingle's book *Blood Sacrifice and the Nation* was published in 1999; in it they argue that the USA possesses at its heart a kind of sacrificial culture that helps bind the states together. The sacrificial system is headed by the President, is symbolized in the flag and enacted through the death of soldiers in warfare. It is their shed blood that is the sacrifice. They see the military – especially in its prime male soldiers – as a special training to kill and be killed. These are people who are 'death-touchers' and are bound together by an honour code. To have failed in a war, as in Vietnam, is deemed a shame and throws a shadow upon this very system of social life. We could, in fact, strengthen their analysis by seeing how the USA often identifies itself as God's chosen people leading the world into truth and the proper way of life which is, essentially, that of American democracy. While this is, of course, one interpretation of events, it allows numerous aspects of life to fall into one broad explanation. The daily pledge of allegiance to the flag in American schools would, for example, be unimaginable in most European countries. Similarly, unlike Britain and the death of its soldiers and civil personnel in the service of its empire period and in the two great wars, America tends not to leave its dead where they fall but to bring them home. It is in one of the hundred or more national-military cemeteries in the USA that the dead are, by strong preference, buried and not in 'some corner of a foreign field'. This aspect of military death brings to the dead a high symbolic value; indeed, Marvin and Ingle see in the military funeral – with the flag being specially folded and given back to the family almost as a kind of symbolic baby – a powerful expression of the nation's commitment to giving life to maintain a way of life. Their interpretation of military death provides a very potent balance to Mitford's over-easy critique of commercialized and cosmetic civilian death.


## Ecology

All of these cases show just how open the human corpse is as a medium of expression of different social values. One stream of such values is of particular contemporary interest and centres on ecology. Its roots lie in the mid-nineteenth-century drive for sanitary reform and urban planning that witnessed the birth of modern cremation, originally heralded as a healthy means of disposing of the dead and circumventing overfull and disease-ridden urban cemeteries. By the beginning of the twenty-first century, however, cremation had come to be viewed by some as a potential source of harmful chemical discharge. The nineteenth-century commitment to social hygiene in newly industrialized areas had evolved into a concern for the world at large, especially with the atmosphere's ozone layer, the destruction of tropical rain forests, animal and plant species, not to mention issues in genetic engineering and human fertilization.

This shift of concern amounts to a revolution in world-view. It reveals a move from debates about God, religion, authority of church traditions and the eternal destiny of humanity to a pre-occupation with the world as a living space, to ethical activity within it and to the likelihood of its having a sustainable future. The focus of attention shifts from the past to the present and from any eternal future in heaven to a long-term future for humanity on earth. Personal survival and immortality have become subsumed into the survival of the human species amidst other species. The change of emphasis is also associated with a rise in the notion of the 'spirituality' of people rather than their religiosity. This kind of change of world-view carries considerable consequences for humanity's understanding of death.

Here much depends both upon the religious history of countries and many other social and environmental factors. The USA, for example, remained a burial culture throughout the twentieth century as it continued the eighteenth- and nineteenth-century customs of burial favoured by Protestant, Catholic and Jewish communities. Only in the early twenty-first century is the USA increasing its use of cremation. In Europe, cremation was much heralded in the mid- to late nineteenth century and developed relatively rapidly in Protestant areas, with Great Britain becoming the dominant user. Roman Catholic areas came into cremation very slowly, and amidst much dispute, while Greek Orthodoxy has stood adamantly against cremation not only for theological reasons of tradition associated with burial and resurrection but also for political reasons of church–state relations in Greece and for the maintenance of what the church would view as Greek identity.

In terms of broad cultural trends the later twentieth century witnessed a growing interest in ecology. For many believers of several traditions the ecological shift of cultural awareness has demanded various forms of eco-theology, with Christian theologians, for example, responding to the criticism that biblical religion encouraged a cavalier attitude to the world, using it as something of a lesser order. In their response theologians speak of the call to stewardship of God's earth as a proper endeavour for Christians. Just how Christians will play the card of ecology alongside the card of heaven remains to be seen. For increasing numbers of people, however, perhaps even for some religious believers, the ecological focus is likely to dominate over, and even replace, previous religious preoccupations with heaven.

## Hope Springs Eternal

Hope, the crucial dynamic presence underlying religious belief, worship and ethics, is also evident in explicitly secular ecological concerns. Hope seems to be part of the drive lying behind humans both in their self-consciousness and in their desire to survive. Inevitably, it would seem, hope plays a major part in ecological concerns whether or not they are given any traditional religious identification. Hope sets itself against the despair that is poised to fall upon those worried over global warming, genetic engineering and other potential hazards to life. Although it is seldom put in such words, it is as though increasing numbers of people are fearing for the death of the planet. Science and technology are, at one and the same time, the basis of pessimism and optimism, of destruction if genetic engineering goes wrong and industrial development overheats the planet, and of optimism if it helps regulate or reverse these adverse features. After the Cold War, the apparent demise of the fear of nuclear destruction has been replaced by a fear of a slower destruction of the world.

In and through ecology individuals have had held out to them a new way of thinking about themselves, their lives and their world. This perspective avoids both the more speculative elements of religion concerning an afterlife and the numerous and often contradicting doctrinal formulae of churches and religions. It presents something more concrete and apparently 'real'. Ecological–environmental ideas, then, can furnish one means of framing human identity and thinking about life. Just how pervasive and satisfying that perspective will prove to be remains unclear at present, but as pressure groups such as Greenpeace or Friends of the Earth and many others influence politicians it is likely to become increasingly persuasive. The very fact that a 'Green Party' presents candidates in political elections in increasing numbers of countries is some evidence for this change.

It is against that background that Great Britain, for example, witnessed a slow but clear interest in funerary rites described in terms of natural burial, green burial or woodland burial as the twentieth century ended. This trend reflects what might be seen as an ecological framing of identity, one that produces its own form of secular eschatology, or doctrine of the 'last things', as it expresses concern for the future of the planet. This outlook may well, for example, turn against cremation on the basis of its gas production and on its removal of the body from its native earth. By contrast, if I give my body back to the earth I am expressing a hope for the future of the planet: this is no longer only a self-related hope of survival but one that also ponders future generations. In another sense this perspective does echo a retrospective fulfilment of identity if people also see such a funeral as reflecting the way a person had lived, their life-values of ecology now being reflected in their death-values. For these may well be people who have, for example, practised recycling of their household waste; they may have sponsored various conservation projects and have held ideological views on, say, vegetarianism. Increasingly in Britain they may be gardeners, committed to the natural relationship between life and death in the cycles of nature. Here we find an echo of John Shotter's sense of the 'relational grammar' of 'what leads to what' in an unbroken sequence in moving around in the places and spaces made available to us by new views of a world. For, just as we learn to 'dwell' in a strange town and to be 'at home' in it, so, too, with a world in which the values of survival are changing (1998: 198).

Here we re-enter a public value system and are not simply left in the private world of individual wishes. The political world of European politics is one such framework within which environmental concerns are resulting in specific directives on such matters as recycling of household waste. This will increasingly affect every home and the domestic life of families, for daily activities influence ideology and broad public values in a most basic way. Here we encounter ecology as a public value system into which individuals will be drawn and from which they may, in turn, draw their own ideas. Ecology draws from branches of science much as traditional eschatology drew from theology. But ecology is not 'post-modern'; if anything it resembles modernity itself as an overarching story of the way things are and of how we relate to the way things are. It covers how we eat, what we buy and how we die. Here, too, the body assumes new significance. It had been said that in the post-modern context the disappearance of shared values left us only with our bodies. The disappearing soul and the empty church are being replaced by diets, healthy eating and the gymnasium. That kind of analysis was, in part, only half correct, reflecting an attitude that is in the process of change as the body-focus comes to be set within ecological values, scientifically informed.

## Forest

These changes bear strongly upon death rites. In chapter 6 we will discuss the two established options of ecclesiastically controlled funeral rites on the one hand, and rites developed by individuals to express their own sense of meaning in relation to memorializing the dead through cremated remains on the other, including the allied case of the National Memorial Arboretum in Britain as a natural woodland context for memorializing the dead which possesses ecological elements without being solely driven by that environmental motive. For the moment the spotlight falls specifically upon the ecological notion of woodland or 'green' burial, referring to the process of burying a body not in any traditional form of churchyard or civic cemetery but in a variety of contexts such as a field in which trees can be planted above graves to develop into woodland. Similarly, a body may be buried in glades or clearings within established woodlands. In terms of basic principles the body is not buried in coffins or caskets that are made to insulate the dead from the earth but in wickerwork or some material that easily decays and fosters the natural processes of bodily decay. The body may be carried or transported to the actual grave by human effort rather than by hearse to allow a greater degree of personal contact with the dead. The funeral itself is likely to accentuate the naturalness of death and of the return of the body to the earth. As the alternative description of 'green' burial aptly expresses, this kind of funeral is rooted in ecological values and marks the increased interest shown in the natural environment not only by scientists but also by large sections of the public.

## Positive and Negative Dust

Here the traditional Christian burial formula, 'earth to earth, ashes to ashes, dust to dust', becomes paradoxical and accentuates the ideological direction taken by 'green' funerals. Theologically, the 'earth to earth' phrase was taken from the biblical Book of Genesis and its myth telling of the creation and fall of mankind. Because Adam and Eve disobey a divine command and eat of the symbolic tree of the knowledge of good and evil they are subjected to hardship: women in the pain of childbirth and subjection to their husbands, and men in the toil through which they will wrest corn from the earth for food. It is precisely through the sweat of toil that they will be able to eat bread until they, themselves, 'return to the ground' out of which, according to one biblical myth, humanity was itself formed. The primal man, Adam, is told that he is, in fact, dust, and will become dust yet again, after his death: 'dust you are, and to dust you will return' (Genesis 3: 19). Doctrinally, then, 'earth to earth' expresses the double idea embracing both the fact that humanity was made from the same earth as everything else, which, in itself, was a positive statement of identity, and the much more negative fact that because humanity fell into a sinful state of disobedience its destiny was death.

So it was that Milton, in accounting for *Paradise Lost*, has the divine voice address Adam in Eden with the words of judgement – 'know thy birth' – a birth from dust and, now, a deathly return to dust (Milton 2000: 223). Self-knowledge now embraces the knowledge of death in a profound reflexivity. This is, precisely, why Christian funeral liturgies offset the dust of death with the 'sure and certain hope of resurrection' effected through the resurrection of Jesus Christ who is, himself, interpreted as a 'second Adam' whose obedience to God overturns the disobedience of the first Adam. As John Henry Newman's hymn, 'Praise to the Holiest in the height', puts it,

> O loving wisdom of our God!
> When all was sin and shame,
> A second Adam to the fight
> And to the rescue came.

However, quite a different motivating idea lies behind the 'earth to earth' of emergent woodland burials whose ecological concerns reflect something of a potential paradigm shift in the understanding of death, one whose consequences are only beginning to become apparent in the first decade of the twenty-first century. Commitments to the conservation of scarce resources in relation to the survival not only of the human species but also of the world itself come to influence ideas of human death and combine with a sense of the naturalness of life and death. The 'earth' that returns to the earth is not the sinful son or daughter of Adam and Eve but the natural human body that had once been formed by earthy, natural processes, and now continues those processes through its death.

The profoundly significant feature of ecology is that it brings together science, ethics, philosophy, economics and politics in ways that are reminiscent of religion in previous eras. Ecology is a unifying perspective. It runs through numerous parts of school curricula as pupils ponder the apparently accessible images of global warming and holes in the ozone layer while, even at a very young age, children have shown interest in the decline of some animals, as with pandas, which the World Wildlife Fund took as its symbolic animal, one with real appeal to children. Younger generations from, approximately, the 1970s were encouraged to think of animal and plant species as precious resources that can never be regained once they are destroyed. Ecology is not, however, a subject restricted to school but, as already mentioned, it impinges upon family and community life through the regular recycling of domestic and community waste. Individuals and families are, increasingly, not only set to think about what they do with waste vegetable matter, waste glass and other domestic refuse, but they are also encouraged to act on their thought, having to ponder in which containers to deposit these various elements of rubbish for public collection.

## Ethics and Spirituality at Large

As these scientific concerns over the environment combine with the pragmatic features of domestic activity, the food-supply, the issue of genetic engineering and the medical opportunities associated with gene therapy and the challenges of cloning, the realm of ethics suddenly emerges in an almost spontaneous fashion. Indeed, the closing decades of the twentieth century witnessed the rise of ethics in an almost unanticipated manner. While ethics had, for centuries, been addressed as a major element of theology and the religious life and, to a more limited extent, of formal philosophical studies, it now opened up as an arena in which all might participate.

Concurrently, another topic that had long been defined in explicitly religious terms, that of 'spirituality', broke loose from ecclesiastical confines to be widely adopted as a valuable concept to describe the depth and quality of life (McGinn 1993). As the twenty-first century began, 'spirituality' had become a popular notion in at least three constituencies lying beyond the immediately ecclesiastical. First, some theologians wished to integrate their own sense of faith with their academic subjects to speak of the importance of a lived embodiment of belief. Second, groups lying beyond established churches in new religious movements spoke of their own endeavours in terms of their spirituality. Third, amongst those engaged in therapy and the palliative care of the sick the notion of spirituality developed as a mode of reflection upon the quality of life that might be pursued by those coming to the end of their days. It now remains for the field of death and bereavement to follow in this path and develop some explicit forms of spirituality of death as a means of focusing and giving voice to experience, emotion and self-reflection in the face of death and to do it with a positive valuation. For, and this is important, the whole development of the notion of 'spirituality' in the three areas specified above has been rooted in a positive spirit.

## Death's Paradigm Shift

Ecology, ethics and spirituality easily found themselves creative complements in emergent views of life taking shape outside traditional churches. Paradoxically, this emergent perspective coexists in many people's lives alongside a consumerist outlook framed by a sense of personal freedom and individualism. Integral to this increased personalizing of life is the desire that life should be lived in as intelligible and authentic a way as possible but not necessarily in terms of established religious ideas. And it is precisely at this point that death encounters its paradigm shift. As significant numbers of individuals no longer believe in life after death, they are less amenable to accepting traditional rites simply because they are traditional. It is extremely likely that the doctrinally informed words of funeral services have become increasingly more dissonant than consonant with the actual beliefs of thousands of people making use of the funeral services of churches. For as long as it was customary, socially expected and organizationally convenient to have a priest conduct a funeral, the great majority of the public took that route. One change of direction in the decades surrounding the emergence of the twenty-first century lay in an increasing personalizing of funerals on the part of many priests as they paid more attention to the past life of the deceased, to their character and interests. Readings from non-biblical sources, and music that might be drawn from the private repertoire of the deceased, are often used alongside or instead of religiously traditional forms. More than that, the opportunity of using non-religious funeral officiants is growing. Here a contemporary consumerist lifestyle comes to underlie funerals, just as it had, slightly earlier, also influenced marriage.

## Ecological Immortality

One way of describing the shift in the meaning of death implicated in ecological ethics and consumerist individualism could be in terms of ecological immortality. As the issue of waste disposal has come to be a pressing concern of ordinary life, it is not surprising that the disposal of the human body should also come to be seen as part of the same general problem – what to do with the outcome of living? In chapter 6 we present two images of the afterlife. One is the traditional Christian view, described in terms of the eschatological fulfilment of identity, and the other involving the private placing of cremated remains in sites of past personal significance as the retrospective fulfilment of identity. In this present chapter, by contrast, we typify woodland burial in the quite different terms of 'ecological immortality'. This is neither to say that those who undertake woodland burial do not adhere to traditional Christian notions of heaven and its prospective identity, nor that they may not reflect something of a strong retrospective fulfilment of identity for the deceased who may have loved 'nature'. But it is to emphasize a quite different idea, that of the intrinsic relationship between the human body and the world as a natural system within which the ongoingness of life is grounded in the successive life and death of individual animals and plants, indeed, of all things. Here we have a world-view that is relatively integrated and intelligible to many contemporary people. It emerges from an interplay between science of an intuitively acceptable kind and a sense of self that is not dependent upon either belief in an otherworldly afterlife nor the fragility of the enduring memories of one's descendants. There is, as it were, something obviously 'real' about the human body returning to the earth and contributing to the mass of living organisms. At the same time, cremation can no longer claim to be the best 'hygienic' method of disposing of corpses, as described in the previous chapter. If traditional Christian ideas of burial in 'sure and certain hope of the resurrection' generated a degree of dissonance amongst those present at funerals but who did not believe in those doctrines, then woodland burial could foster an assonant authenticity as the dead are given back to 'nature'. The key to the appeal of this outlook lies in a dynamic view of 'nature', of an ongoing system of which one is a part and not of some radical divide between mankind and nature. Similarly, an ecological sense of identity brings an additional value to the realm of private language and individual memory that so easily surrounds the secret placing of ashes in a shared and loved spot. In other words, woodland burial furnishes an authentic basis for understanding both life and death for those for whom either 'heaven' or 'memory' is an unbelievable or inadequate means of making sense of life and of death.

As already intimated above, one intriguing aspect of such woodland burial, and of the ecological life and death-styles allied with it, is the way it contradicts the general notion of post-modernism. The oft-repeated definition of post-modernism denies any overarching and shared interpretation of life in order to stress the individualized and self-originated meaning of things. While the shared credal beliefs of established religions in many parts of Europe and beyond have fragmented, and while some individuals may have adopted something of an individualized, self-constructed, idiosyncratic outlook on life, it remains the case that many have come to share in the scientifically informed notion of ecology. To reinforce a point also made above, along with this scientific perspective has gone a renewed interest in ethics and the responsibility of society in both fostering and moderating research into, and the exploitation of, ecological issues such as genetic engineering or human cloning. It remains to be seen just how widespread this form of coping with human remains will become in replacing either cremation or traditional forms of burial but, certainly, it presents a major change in belief and practice as far as the history of death is concerned.

Plate 1 Stockholm crematorium interior
Main Chapel of Stockholm's renowned Woodland Cemetery Crematorium by Architect Gunnar Asplund (1885–1940). Fresco *Life-Death-Life* by Sven Erixson.

Plate 2 Stockholm crematorium exterior sculpture close-up
Sculpture, *The Resurrection*, by Joel Lundquist, depicts the upward journey of the self in death's conquest. Art's role in human reflection on destiny.

Plates 3 and 4 Bordeaux Crematorium interior with no symbols (above) and with crucifix and candles (below)
Together these depict the sacred–secular option modern crematoria offer to individuals by the use or absence of religious symbols.

Plate 5 Golders Green Crematorium, marble memorial
Memorial plaques significant given the likely absence of gravestones over ashes.

Plate 6 Auschwitz, a memorial
A call to the world to assert memory in a camp that sought to obliterate Jewish identity.

Plates 7, 8 and 9 Three exhibits from a 1996 Amsterdam exhibition mounted by Harry Heyink and Walter Carpey.
(7) Back-pack coffin: Symbolic portrayal of death's immediacy: we ever carry it with us. (8) Eco-friendly grave products and (9) Informal body packing expressing the affinity of ecological lifestyle and death-style.

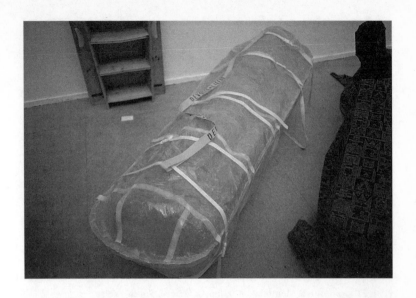

Plate 10 Memorial Day in rural Utah
Annual Memorial Day in May with families tending graves in a strongly
traditional and burial-focused society.

Plate 11 Communal Memorial, Aberfan Cemetery, South Wales
Architecture expressing unity in loss and grief.

Plate 12 Gravestone: Hungary
Artistic expression of individuality of a self amidst the communal tradition of burial.

# Chapter 5

# Art, Literature and Music

This chapter suggests ways in which the immense volume and variety of the world's artistic, literary and musical compositions allow hope to play its part within human responses to mortality. Together they frustrate death in having the 'last word' on life. Here we highlight parts of the Bible and illustrate its dramatic impact on human ideas of life and death as in Dante and Milton's literature and Handel's music. We then complement those religious trends with some secular responses to death. Although the power of language, art and song underlying self-reflection makes grief all the more poignant, it also fosters our ability to cope with bereavement. The self-awareness underlying human life and its drive for meaning combines with optimism to produce hope and the motivation that enables people to set out, purposefully, on their culture-building way. Sooner or later, however, all are confronted by the death of those who make our world meaningful and, through those deaths, hope is challenged.

Whatever it was that prompted earliest humans to treat their dead in some formal way, it is obvious that they generally did not simply discard them. Whether or not the religious traditions of humanity arose as an evolutionary response to death we will never know. What is sure is that religious aspects of life developed a strong sense of responsibility towards death. In cultures where religion became an easily identifiable social domain it assumed major significance in addressing mortality – in speaking words against death. I would even argue that humanity became stronger because of its death-awareness than it would have, had people simply discarded the dead as so much rubbish. Grief was inevitable in the closely bonded small groups that characterized much early human society. As social and intelligent beings, always ready to adapt to new challenges, humans acted corporately to cope with grief and, in so doing, generated a ritual response to death with all the integrating effect of such an endeavour. This included the mythological and theological explanations that came to serve not only the purpose in hand but also a higher purpose, viz., the provision of explanation of the meaning of life itself. To say this is, of course, speculative since it lays the broader doctrines of religion on the shoulders of death-conquest and it is perfectly possible – though not entirely likely – that religions emerged for quite different or additional reasons. Be that as it may, it was through ritual and myth linking death and life, and in the art and architecture of memorial sites, that human beings had opportunity to recall the dead and their past events, and to gain a perspective upon life and the future.

## Variety

Music, art and literature are all media in and through which human creativity addresses the joys and sorrows of life and, in so doing, offers a means of transcending the limitations those constraints seem to impose. The choice of such death-defying compositions in these cultural domains is immense. We might, for example, move from the Venerable Bede's seventh-century history of the English-speaking people to the twentieth-century novelist Darryl Pinckney in a relatively easy step. Bede tells how the devout nun Begu was granted a vision of the death of St Hilda. Awakened by a bell, Begu 'saw the roof open, and a great light pour from above. While she gazed . . . she saw the soul of God's servant Hilda borne up to heaven in the midst of light accompanied and guided by angels' (Bede 1955: 244). Pinckney's novel, by sharp contrast, tells of an aunt Clara who fancied instructing that her ashes be 'put in one of Nida Lee's hollowed out flamingos' or be discreetly scattered 'in the aisles at Rich's Department Store', reflecting a stronger sense of this-worldly consumerism than the other-worldly asceticism of Hilda and Begu (Pinckney 1992: 39).

## Bible

Hardly a novel and scarcely any biography, secular or hagio-graphic, completes its account of human life without adding some element to the history of death. Underlying many of them is the Bible itself, a foundational source of human self-reflection, as described in the previous chapter on Adam and Eve. As the biblical narrative proceeds it describes the deaths of patriarchs, including Jacob who is embalmed according to Egyptian custom and buried in Canaan after appropriate mourning (Genesis 50: 1–14). Moses can praise God for the devastation of his enemies (Exodus 15: 1–18), but also transmit the divine commandment, 'Thou shalt not kill', which is perhaps better rendered 'not commit murder' (Exodus 20: 13). The evolution of a temple with its priesthood and cult of sacrifice brought together a cluster of ideas in which the death of an animal represented and substituted for the death of a person in an act of atonement between God and humanity (Leviticus 16: 5–19). At other times people die as a result of their own wickedness, disobedience or because they are enemies (Deuteronomy 20: 17). Personal grief also holds its place, as when king David weeps for his son Absalom (2 Samuel 19: 1), or when Job has his entire family destroyed and responds by saying that he had come from the womb naked and would die naked. Then, in words that stood for centuries within some Christian funeral rites, he resigns himself by saying 'the Lord giveth and the Lord taketh away; blessed be the name of Lord' (Job 1: 21). Within the book of Psalms, too, there are very many reflections upon death and expressions of faithful hope despite life's hardship, as in Psalm twenty-three whose opening words, 'The Lord is my shepherd', have become so familiar as a funeral hymn. In the Apocrypha – texts accepted as scripture by some but not all Christians – the faithful are told to weep bitterly when immediately bereaved but then to be comforted, and to remember that 'grief may result in death' and too much sorrow does good neither to the dead nor to the living (Sirach 38: 16–23).

But it is in the New Testament that death becomes absolutely central and the prime foundation laid for subsequent Christian history that would influence the art, literature and music of western-rooted cultures for millennia. The life of Jesus involves miracles in which the dead are raised to life, as with the story of Lazarus which included the words 'I am the resurrection and the life. Those who believe in me, even though they die, will live', words repeated at innumerable funeral services (John 11: 125). Still, it is the death of Jesus through crucifixion that became central to the narrative, indeed to the way Christians came to read and interpret the whole Bible, to develop their art, literature and hymnody. Images of animal sacrifice now gain new meaning in his death as a sacrifice for the sin of the world, the bitterness and the comfort of the Psalms are echoed in him, and through the evolving ritual of the Mass, Eucharist or Holy Communion, his sacrificial death is reckoned to be offered anew or recalled by faith. His death is believed to embrace the death of all people but, more than that, his resurrection from the dead becomes the basis of hope of resurrection life for all. The history of the death of Jesus – always complemented by belief in his resurrection – contributed more to the history of the world than the death of any other figure. Every church in every country attests to it, with its meaning being elaborated and developed not only in formal theology and liturgy but also in literature of a more secular kind.

## Dante

Amongst such, none in western thought is more elaborate than that of Dante Alighieri (1265–1321). Born in Florence, his spiritual epic-poem *Divine Comedy* furnishes a distinctive commentary upon life, death and the afterlife. From one perspective it is its own kind of pilgrim's progress, from another a Christian 'book of the dead'. Though more a reflection for the living than either a guide for the dying or a manual for priests – as with the Tibetan and Egyptian books of the dead – his three realms of hell, purgatory and paradise offer vivid visions of spiritual possibilities. *Divine Comedy* was prompted, in part at least, by the death of a close friend, Beatrice, when the 25-year-old Dante was 'overcome by grief at her loss' (Musa, M. 1984: 20). In its first volume, 'The Inferno', Dante reflects on sin, evil and punishment, providing a vivid verbal account that would be reflected in many later scenes of hellish pain and torment. Some of these depict souls engulfed in flame or having their feet permanently burnt, whilst Judas Iscariot – the disciple who betrayed Jesus – is constantly chewed with his body inside and legs kicking-out from one of the three mouths of Lucifer, the great centre of the underworld who is, himself, half frozen in eternal ice. Other sinners are depicted suffering in a wasteland of burning sand upon which 'broad flakes of fire showered steadily', or in a frozen lake of ice with teeth clicking notes as from 'storks' beaks snapping shut'. The ordinary symbolism of hot and cold objects is inverted or intensified to dramatize sinners' experience of them. The scenes encountered by our pilgrim are recounted in sufficient detail to help furnish the medieval mind with terrible images to ponder when considering death and its hinterland, even when that land was entirely framed by a Christian providence and possessed heaven as its ultimate destination.

## Milton

Several centuries later John Milton, one of the most creative English minds of the seventeenth century, also engaged with death. Though involved in debates on international and national politics, his religious sense granted mortality a central place, not least because death touched him deeply as reflected in the poem *Lycidas*, composed on the death of a friend. Later in life the death of his wife was juxtaposed to his own loss of eyesight. Whether in his complex and difficult relations with his wife or in his shift between religious denominations, Milton pursued the goal of a truthful understanding of life. Never was this as apparent as in *Paradise Lost*, his theological epic narrative, where he attempts to justify the ways of God to men. At the heart of this extensive account of the temptation and fall of Adam, with all the dark and shameful repercussions of the natural and heavenly realms, lies death. Milton's reflections on death, as immediately focused upon the Fall of Adam as they are, nevertheless remain many-faceted and extend into the wider crises and self-questionings of men and women. He puts into Adam's mouth words that many others have uttered or entertained as painful thoughts. Adam, lost for the moment in a sense of despair and shame, asks, 'Why comes not death . . . to end me . . . But death comes not at call' (Milton 2000: 240). As many have done when in despair, he too longs for death but his deep desire remains unmet. He protests that he did not ask to be made and asks why he is, as it were, mocked by death: 'Did I require thee, Maker, from my clay to mould me man . . . That dust I am, and shall to dust return: O welcome hour whenever! . . . why do I overlive, Why am I mocked with death, and lengthened out To deathless pain? how gladly would I meet Mortality my sentence, and be earth insensible, how glad would lay me down as in my mother's lap!' (Milton 2000: 237–8). This echoes many who long for death, especially when seen as all too slow in coming. Here, too, is an echo of Dante's wretches who 'have no hope of truly dying', and who were the mediocrities of uncommitted and tediously selfish lives and, because of that, were 'deprived of life and death at once' (Dante, 1984: 91, 380. Canto III 46, XXXIV 27). Milton even suggests mutual suicide as a means of preventing children being brought into such a woeful life: 'Let us seek Death, or he not found, supply With our own hands his office on ourselves . . . and have the power of many ways to die the shortest choosing' (Milton 2000: 243). Adam, however, having picked up a sense of future possibilities, will no longer have 'violence against ourselves' mentioned and sojourns on even though he will, yet, encounter many shocks, as when he sees Cain kill Abel and grasps the nature of death in hard reality: 'But have I now seen death? Is this the way I must return to native dust? O sight of terror, foul and ugly to behold. Horrid to think, how horrible to feel!' The Archangel Michael responds to Adam, telling him that, in fact, there are 'many shapes of death, and many are the ways that lead to this grim cave, all dismal', and reveals a place where many die of many causes, physical and mental (Milton 2000: 259). Adam wonders how man, made in God's image, could come to such ignominious forms of death; truly it would be better not to have been born! The angel does give one word of advice to Adam, and it is of a self-control that might appeal to some modern ears, 'The rule of *Not too much*, by temperance taught in what thou eat'st and drink'st', and by this rule of temperance humans may live long and death will come when 'like ripe fruit thou drop into thy mother's lap' (Milton 2000: 261. Original emphasis). This 'rule of temperance', well known in classical antiquity from Horace, was explicitly contradicted in the mid-nineteenth century by Søren Kierkegaard as part of his extensive analysis of *The Sickness unto Death* (1968) to which we return in chapter 7. Milton, however, through the emotional and spiritual spectrum of *Paradise Lost*, describes some human views of death, from deep despair, shame and thoughts of suicide, to an acknowledgement of the accident of birth and one's unsought-for presence in this world, to death at the close of a full and relatively well-lived life. Though framed by a broad Christian doctrinal view of life, Milton still manages to capture key popular attitudes that are far less traditionally theological but, nevertheless, heartfelt by those who have to make their life on earth.

## Secular Strains

Indeed, the literature of the world often maintains a steady current of death concern, though this is not always on the theme of conquest but of that deep seriousness of reflection that language enables us to formulate. Here three quite different examples must suffice in cases that some might find incongruous. The first is from Shakespeare's *Sonnets*, the second from J. K. Rowling's Harry Potter stories and the third from Ewan McColl's folk-songs.

Shakespeare, a brief generation before Milton, addresses death in many of its modes, though here I identify only his thoughts on the loss of love. In Sonnet sixty-six he reflects on life as filled with thwarted ideals and, tired of false shows, would gladly anticipate the rest that comes through death were it not for the fact that one must leave one's loved one behind:

> Tired with all these, from these would I be gone,
> Save that to die, I leave my love alone.

And he would wish no enduring grief for the surviving lover, rather the deceased should be forgotten as quickly as the ringing of the parish church's death-knell ceases. He loves so much that he wishes no pain to be occasioned by his memory, as Sonnet seventy-seven advises:

No longer mourn for me when I am dead
Than you shall hear the surly sullen bell
Give warning to the world that I am fled
From this vile world with vilest worms to dwell . . .

When I, perhaps, compounded am with clay,
Do not so much as my poor name rehearse,
But let your love even with my life decay.

This desired forgetfulness is summarized in Sonnet seventy-two, 'After my death, dear love, forget me quite'. Many of these sentiments find echoes in contemporary experience, when individuals come to a point at which they do not fear death itself, especially if life and its demands have become too pressing, but they do care about those they will leave behind. Poetic expressions of love and loss have become increasingly important in contemporary life, especially when families and friends wish to see a funeral as a reflection upon, and even a celebration of, the life of the dead. Whether or not in compensation for widespread decrease of knowledge of the Bible and empathy with its formulation of the human condition, many find poetry a valuable way of expressing grief, love, hope or hopelessness.

In prose, too, not least in children's literature, the treatment of death finds its place, as in J. K. Rowling's Harry Potter, now read worldwide by millions of children – and indeed adults – with translations including Welsh and Latin. The portrayal of the experience of grief in *Harry Potter and the Prisoner of Azkaban*, for example, presents a particularly insightful set of adventures. At one perilous point the teenage Harry thinks he has seen his dead father for whom he longs. He discloses this to his deeply respected headmaster, Dumbledore, saying he knows 'it was stupid thinking it was him . . . I mean, I knew he was dead'. The headmaster replies both rhetorically and with advice: 'You think the dead we have loved ever truly leave us? You think that we don't recall them more clearly than ever in times of great trouble?

Your father is alive in you, Harry, and shows himself most plainly when you have need of him' (Rowling 1999: 460). This same adventure features a category of evil beings called Dementors who 'glory in decay and despair, they drain peace, hope and happiness out of the air around them', and render their prey 'soulless . . . left with nothing but the worst experiences of . . . life' (Rowling 1999: 204). These Dementors highlight the importance of hope in all reflections upon death, and to have such a name and a creative description of these negative experiences is highly valuable indeed; we will return to hope at the close of this chapter.

## Art

Away from written texts, one of the strangest of all human responses to death is to be found in paintings of the dead. Death masks, too, shaped from the corpse's face, have held occasional interest. The very existence of an art of death is of fundamental cultural importance, not simply because it depicts both the public and the deeply private expression of grief, but because it is painted at all. One of the distinctive features of human self-reflection lies in the fact that we paint things that we can also see for ourselves. Why paint what can be seen directly? Why own a painting of a place, for example, if one sees the actual location every day? One obvious reason lies in the process of creative representation – it is because we think about and ponder things and do not simply observe them. And in thinking of them we 'add to' their significance in creating multi-layered meanings.

So it is that statues, paintings and, later still, photographs of the dead have played a significant part in the history of human reflection. This has been especially important for Christian reflection upon the death of Christ. Spreading from Italy from the mid-thirteenth century, for example, religious art increasingly depicted the passion and death of Jesus in increasingly realistic ways. This was largely under the influential patronage of the Franciscan Order whose founder, Francis of Assisi (1181–1226), had manifested the stigmata – the signs of Christ's crucifixion – and fostered a new emphasis of spirituality that dwelt upon Christ's suffering and death (Derbes 1996: 18). In a more secular context, from the fourteenth century onwards, we find increasing numbers of European effigies of influential people, monarchs, soldiers and bishops depicted, often in the chapels of great churches, wearing their insignia of office. Sometimes those symbols of earthly influence are set against the fact of death, as when the clothed effigies have placed at a lower level, beneath them, skeletal effigies – life above and death below symbolizing the marks of status and the realities of mortality. Even when no such skeleton appears, some symbol of mortality, especially skulls, is regularly incorporated in the art and memorials of the dead.

There is, of course, no certainty that as twenty-first-century readers we know how people of other times and places feel about life and death; the most we can do is acknowledge their concern. In a most insightful and fully illustrated study Michael Camille explored the late medieval images of death by Pierre Remiet, a little-known artist and illustrator, to suggest that death was a general frame for embodied life and not some philosophical end-point that provides 'the foundation of human identity and selfhood' as some contemporary philosophers postulate (Camille 1996: 245). But, as Camille noted, there are inevitable differences in the way death is viewed when life is seen as a pilgrimage ending in an afterlife than when this life is all.

As the western world changed from medieval to Renaissance moods and perspectives, pictorial art followed. In sixteenth- and seventeenth-century Netherlands, for example, individuals used their wealth to depict their dead relatives, not least their children. Sometimes these children are shown, fairly realistically, as dead babies, but sometimes they are given the form and setting of angelic beings. Less domestically and much more scientifically, art also comes to depict the scientific role of medicine as a practice involved with the dead body, as in Rembrandt's famous anatomy class of 1632 in which the medical instructor dissects part of body surrounded by some seven pupils. In the foreground stands an open book, adding an authoritative validity to their work; similarly, van der Maes's painting of joined Siamese twins is set against the background of an anatomy theatre (Sliggers 1998: 25, 211). This form of death art can be seen as expressing an early form of the medicalization of death, the sense that the developing medical profession possesses a right to engage with dead bodies and not leave them to the strict control of the Church.

From the later part of the nineteenth century the emergence of photography added the possibility of direct representation of the dead, in which earlier artistic embellishments of skeletal realism or angelic idealism in portraying babies, for example, gave way to an immediacy of death. These give the living a concrete focus for their changing memories and take us into the domain of private grief, one example of which, that of Picasso, grants some limited insight into this twentieth-century artistic genius's deep private grief as it intersected with the public world of art. While his character paves the way for our consideration of the fear of death in chapter 7, it shows here how his creativity combined with a charismatic personality, giving the world an uncompromising, conflict-ridden individual who needed to pour out his personal grief whilst also seeking to insulate his inner-self from prying eyes. The death of his eight-year-old sister when he was but fourteen deeply affected Picasso. When she was dying of diphtheria he sought to bargain with God, offering to sacrifice his life's ambition as an artist if her life was saved. A few years later, the death of two of his closest friends led to a series of paintings 'through which he sought to exorcise the pain and guilt' of loss (Stassinopoulos Huffington 1988: 30, 55). Titles such as *The Kiss of Death*, *The Cry of Death* and the *Presence of Death* all reflect what has been called his black period, his time of being haunted by death.

## Portraying the Dead

Most ordinary folk do not have the luxury of being able to paint in response to death. Whatever their private thoughts may be, the public world stands as the arena in which those relationships have to be expressed, catching as best it may the nuances of personal experience. Thus stands the gravestone: marker of a public life and private memories. At the beginning of the twenty-first century in Britain this is an object undergoing dramatic change in presenting portraits of the dead person. There are at least two routes – historical and cultural – from the gravestone with its plain wording of name, dates of birth and death, kinship ties and, often, a biblical text to the gravestone as a frame for a photograph of the deceased person, taken when alive.

The historical route tells of Italian and Polish migrant settlers in Britain, very largely Roman Catholic, and largely post Second World War, who finally died in Britain and whose adult children sought to bury them according to familiar rites of their homeland. Thus it was that photographs of the dead – often imported from producers in Italy – were placed upon gravestones in the second half of the twentieth century. This was more easily done in local-authority-controlled cemeteries than in churchyards controlled by the Church of England which, until very recently, maintained an aesthetic of gravestones that favoured neither such picturing of the dead nor what it might regard as florid eulogy. Even the name 'Dad' has been frowned upon by some local Church authorities. While the Church could filter 'foreign' culture, local authorities were, of necessity, more permeable.

The cultural route adds another dimension and marks a particular shift in British culture, from illiteracy, through literacy in text to 'literacy' in visual imagery. The nineteenth century witnessed a dramatic increase in literacy which was not divorced from Christianity, especially in its Protestant form which fostered the growth and expansion of bible, tract and missionary societies all advocating personal bible reading. This was also the period of rapid urbanization, population growth and the rise of civic cemeteries. Now, for the first time, increasing numbers of the population would have their grave marked and, as often as not, have some biblical text inscribed upon it. In the USA the American Civil War of the 1860s with its 600,000 dead led to a statutory right to an individual tomb and a written record of the dead person's identity (Petrucci 1998: 117). The two great world wars produced similar memorials, both individual and corporate. In the First World War, for example, approximately half of the million British dead received marked, personal, graves and half unmarked graves with corporate memorials (Davies 2002: 159). In British culture gravestones became normative, now located more often in civic cemeteries than in churchyards yet still marked with brief biographical details and, most often, a biblical text or generalized poetic expression about an afterlife or some future meeting in heaven. They were the Protestant dead, even if in civic cemeteries.

Although the photograph had existed for a century or more, it was relatively slow in moving from professional to amateur use but its growth during the final thrust of visual culture from the mid-1980s into the early 1990s cannot be ignored. As part of this visual world, even the ultrasound images of unborn babies have come into prominence in a world of rare and economically demanding pregnancies. Then, too, came the photographing of the relatively rare neonatal deaths of babies. In some hospitals parents came to be encouraged to hold their dead baby and to be photographed together, though there is a difference of professional opinion over whether this helps subsequent adaptation to this early bereavement. Still, this hospital-focused yet domestic aspect of picturing the dead speaks volumes on the power of photographic possibility in relation to private memory. It also underscores the profound rise in significance of neonatal deaths in the later twentieth century.

For adult deaths it is one thing to have still photographs but quite another to have them moving and talking on video recordings. With video and film the memory of the dead becomes more dynamic. And it was from approximately 1990 that requests for photographs of the dead for addition to their gravestones began to grow from British families not of Catholic-Continental origin. Inspiration from those Catholic sources was important, as might have been advertisement from companies interested in developing this business. Glasgow, with its strong Catholic population, was one centre of growth, so was Edinburgh and parts of Lancashire. Birmingham and London, though each with mixed communities, followed suit. Some Muslims, too, saw this as an appropriate way of marking their dead. Jews, largely, did not, given a degree of prohibition upon representing the human form. This option seems to go, for example, with people who die young, say young men involved in accident or tragedy and who tend to be buried rather than cremated. Distinctions between Catholic and Protestant ethos gave way to consumerist preference in a broad secular world of private sentiment. Lifestyle was reflected in style of death – at least in form and memorial.

That itself offers a clue to memorial-photographs. By the opening years of the twenty-first century over 70 per cent of Britons were cremated, with an increasing percentage of cremated remains not being buried and given a grave marker on which an image might be carried, but placed on sites of personal significance: a British trend that is datable to approximately 1974. Those who are buried tend to have explicitly chosen that form of funeral, perhaps for family reasons or, for example, when the death has been unexpected, accidental or tragic. In such cases relatives often view cremation as inappropriate because it adds a further degree of 'removal' of the dead to the already unexpected death. It is precisely to mark and cope with this rupture of experience that graves afford a concrete place of memory that is something more than merely personal and private. The dead are not wiped off the surface of social life and personal memory but are given a formal cemetery location. Cremation, by contrast, can in such cases be regarded as 'too final'. The placing of images of the dead on gravestones does, however, allow a higher degree of personal memory and, in some ways, complements the public place of the grave. In the case of babies and even of still-births, however, the image represents anticipated hope rather than recall of past mutual experience, except that of the pregnancy and its earlier hopes.

European artistic culture has, from at least the fourteenth century, furnished representations of the dead whether in death masks or paintings, their images serving social status as much as private grief. Victoria, Queen Empress, was painted in just this fashion by Hubert von Herkomer, Ruskin's successor as Slade Professor at Oxford, and frequent illustrator of the *Graphic* magazine. On 24 January 1901 Herkomer painted the Queen as she lay dead. Surrounded by flowing and airy muslins, small florets and several lilies, her face alone is visible but for her right hand which holds a cross (Edwards 1999: 95). At last she would lie alongside her long-dead and much-grieved spouse, having given his image to Britain and the world in the Royal Albert Hall and the Albert Memorial – enduring structures long outlasting whatever were her transient inner-pictures of her lover-prince. Such works reflect the style of the age and the capacity of the sponsor.

The emergence of late twentieth- and early twenty-first-century society in Britain marks similar cultural opportunities framed by economic possibilities and the availability of cultural forms. Britain, it would seem, has begun to appreciate the popular Catholic photograph at just the time when companies can make use of computer processes of scanning photographs and other rapid means of reproducing them in ceramic images. Unlike earlier, hand-coloured, sepia tints that faded under the ultra-violet light of the sun, the new techniques are durable. What Britain has not done, to any extensive degree, is copy the American 'portraiture' of the dead in its cosmetic form of life-like corpses. Whatever other images of the dead have been espoused in the USA, that of the inviolable corpse, looking well and simply sleeping, safe in its casket and later in its reinforced concrete grave, has not been desired. Human imagination, in Britain, prefers to remain with the memory of the deceased as they were in life, and as photography can so well reflect, and not with the dead, not even the cosmetic dead. While some groups with family members, for example, in the Indian subcontinent might wish to video-record their dead and their funerals, to enable other relatives to know just what has happened, in Britain the still photograph takes precedence, even though it may have been selected through an aroused consciousness of the visual brought about by video-camera ownership.

## Religious Fusion

Nevertheless, it is within the life of religious traditions that representations of the dead have, traditionally, most intimately combined with music, art, literature and music in the process of death-conquest, passing beyond mere 'words against death' to present a domain in which the 'last enemy', in the words of Christianity's St Paul, is overcome. As argued above, Christianity affirms Jesus as Christ the Victor of death as enshrined at the heart of the ritual of the Eucharist celebrated in church buildings which, in themselves, symbolize the doctrine of the resurrection. Tombs of the dead exist within older churches and many more outside: traditionally the altars of Catholic churches contained a relic of a martyr. Indeed, tradition could even describe the altar as Christ's tomb prior to the miracle of transubstantiation. Inscriptions upon ordinary graves express the hope of eternal life through Christ and the prayers uttered at those altars work on the assumption of life after death. The light pervading such churches often filters through stained glass windows that, like the liturgical account structuring the Eucharist, tell the story of salvation history. People enter into these beliefs through what they say as through what they do, as when eating sacramental bread and drinking wine to participate in the sacrificed life of Christ which is also an assurance of their own eternal destiny.

Music adds to death-conquest through its capacity to foster transcendence even in what might be described as the 'ordinary' secular level of life. Music activates the brain and possesses the potential to give the hearer a sense of being transported 'out of this world' into a state of timelessness. If this is true, as many find it to be, in the ordinary sphere of life it becomes even more potent when aligned with beliefs of eternity. The spectrum of sensation afforded by music passes from its power to console the individual in times of distress, whether for a composer who uses music as a response to grief, as with Buxtehude who deployed his compositional skill to express his feeling of bereavement in his *Lament on the death of his father*, or a grief-stricken relative benefiting from the music of such a composer.

One of the best-known examples of music and words combining in an artistic spirituality of death conquest is that of Handel's *Messiah*. One of his relatively few specifically religious works, its expansive engagement with death exceeds many other pieces of world music. It grounds itself in the Christian view of the Bible as divided into Old and New Testaments in which prophetic hope of a Messiah passes into its realization in the person of Jesus. Handel sets to music this prophetic promise of a Messiah who will not only save people from their sin but will bring about a conquest of death. The soprano aria, 'I know that my Redeemer liveth', coming immediately after the Hallelujah Chorus in praise of the risen Christ who will rule the world, explicitly sets the image of the decayed and worm-eaten human body against the belief 'that in my flesh shall I see God'. The triumph of Christ – risen from the dead – becomes the basis for the believer's resurrection, portrayed as an awaking from sleep. Christ who brings life is then contrasted with Adam who brought death through his disobedience to God: 'for as in Adam all die, even so in Christ will all be made alive'. The exalted confidence in this transformation of death into life is reinforced by the trumpet accompaniment to 'the trumpet shall sound and the dead shall be raised'. The transformation of the dead through the resurrection and into the life of heaven is explained by the need for the corruptible human nature to 'put on incorruption and immortality'. So it is that death is 'swallowed up in victory' and the victory of the grave shown to be ultimately destroyed and then, as the text moves into a tight theological argument about sin and law, it is overwhelmed, almost marginalized, by the lively chorus, 'But thanks, thanks be to God who giveth us the victory through our Lord Jesus Christ'.

The *Messiah* is a particularly interesting Protestant engagement with death, reflecting Handel's Lutheranism, and contrasts with the many musical settings of the Catholic Requiem Masses for the dead that dwell upon the need for divine mercy and forgiveness and upon the hope of not being abandoned by God at death but, rather, asking that divine peace may be given to the departed soul. In the fourteenth and fifteenth centuries such masses also stressed the longstanding idea of the day of wrath that surrounded the dead as they anticipated the day of God's judgement. The Requiem Mass, as its name implies, was an expression of faith that the dead might rest in peace, but it was an expression set within the structure of the Mass itself. In symbolic terms the death of a particular individual was brought into the context of the rite marking the saving death of Jesus Christ. In ordinary Masses the dead are remembered in prayer and the holy dead – the Saints – may also be invoked in prayer, all alongside the priest's memorializing the death of Christ. In formal Catholic theology the sacrificial death of Christ is represented in and through the rite and this brings home to believers the dramatic power of death and of its transcendence, day after day, generation after generation.

In its Protestant outlook and in the fact that it was not a musical accompaniment to any religious service, the *Messiah* was, in other words, not a musical setting of the Mass but a religious oratorio, a musical telling of the gospel story of Christ and of the alliance between Christ and the Christian. It is more of a sung sermon than an enacted Eucharist. Unlike Requiem Masses, too, the *Messiah* is set within a very much larger frame of biblical reference: indeed, it is, essentially, a Protestant biblical reflection on the priesthood of all believers, each possessing a direct alliance with Christ the High Priest who, alone, makes intercession for believers and who replaces the need of intermediary priests on earth. Affirmation replaces intercession. In a touch of theological and musical genius the work moves towards its climax by linking the Old Testament sacrificial lambs of the temple used in the removal of sin with Christ as the Lamb who sits upon the Throne of God as announced in the Book of Revelation, the last book of the New Testament. The climax then comes in the magnificent chorus 'Blessing and Honour and Power be unto Him for ever and ever' and in a final 'Amen' chorus. Since its first performance in 1742 many churches and choral societies have performed this work throughout the world, especially at Christmas and Easter, and in so doing have brought millions to ponder the Christian engagement with divine law, disobedience and the centrality of Jesus of Nazareth whose resurrection conquers death.

No sharper expression of a shift from that Christian hope in eternal life to a contemporary secular view of life's meaning as lying within one's biography and not in one's eternity can be clearly seen than in the folk-song *The Joy of Living*. This deeply evocative song of Ewan McColl, who died in 1989, catches much of what we discussed in chapter 3 on the privatized use of cremated remains as a means of expressing a much-loved relationship, in his case with his partner and singing companion Peggy Seeger as well as with his children and the places he loved. The song bids farewell to the Northern hills and mountains before passing to his personal love. Acknowledging that his time has come, he bids her 'Lie in my arms once more until the darkness comes.' He wants to hold her hand, to join voices and 'sing of the hurt and the pain and joy of living'. He bids farewell to his 'chicks' who soon must 'fly alone'. They are flesh of his flesh, bone of his bone. He wishes that their days may be long and their journey safe for he knows that they bear within them the gift of love. He longs that they may 'savour each new day and the taste of its mouth' as they 'never lose sight of the thrill and the joy of living'. Then, finally,

> Take me to some high place
> Of heather, rock and ling.
> Scatter my dust and ashes,
> Feed me to the wind.
> So that I will be
> Part of all you see,
> The air you are breathing.
> I'll be part of the curlew's cry
> And the soaring hawk,
> The blue milkwort
> And the sundew hung with diamonds.
> I'll be riding the gentle wind
> That blows through your hair,
> Reminding you how we shared
> In the joy of living.

As a Marxist McColl does not speak of any religiously framed eternal life but, like many others, sees his 'future' in the ongoing life of his children and in the memory of his lover, all framed by 'the gentle wind' that 'blows though your hair'. This profoundly personal song possesses tremendous appeal and the capacity to evoke deep responses in those who have their memories of 'the joy of living'. Peggy Seeger, in her introduction to the posthumously published biography of McColl, speaks as though to him: 'Comrade Ewan McColl, I salute you. I love you and miss you. You seem to be in every corner of the house we shared, in every corner of my being' (1990: 6). Her words reflect that awareness of how an identity can be pervaded by the presence of another person. It is deeply existential. This song marks the retrospective sense of fulfilment of identity just as Handel framed the Christian hope of a future fulfilment in heaven.

## Hope

Hope is a recurrent theme in this book; it would not be too much even to suggest that any history of death is, at the same time, a history of hope. With McColl's song hope is shown not as a heavenly path but as finding a home in human reflections upon relationships. Whether in its future orientation or in the past, some form of hope expresses a quality of transcendence, of giving substance to the quality of being human. In chapter 2, for example, we briefly mentioned, in a critical way, Elisabeth Kübler-Ross's influential *On Death and Dying* but there we did not do justice to a major yet often ignored element of her work concerning the place and power of hope in those facing death. If, as much of this book argues, death transcendence is a characteristic of human culture, it is only so because of the nature and outcome of hope as an element of human life, both individual and social. What art, literature and music do, each in their own way, is give expression to hope. They turn the abstract idea of hope into a concrete sentiment. Each medium draws individuals out of themselves and, by showing how others have felt and feel, allows hope to infuse their respective 'words against death', words that, in time, allow the grief-stricken an onward journey.

# Chapter 6

# Places of Memory

Two major topics underlie this chapter, the sense of loss expressed in myths on the origin of death and the sense of hope manifested in places of memory. This latter feature takes up the majority of the chapter and is presented in the form of a specially constructed classification that pairs forms of hope with forms of memorial site.

## Myth

Long before writing emerged, people explained the nature of the world, of life and death, through what we now call myth. The most extensive account of myths concerning death is that of Sir James Frazer, the distinguished Victorian classicist and anthropologist. Though best known for his widely known yet, now, seldom read *Golden Bough*, he also produced several volumes on *The Belief in Immortality and The Worship of the Dead*, originally delivered as the Gifford Lectures at St Andrews University in 1911 and 1912. In these Frazer, in his most beautiful English prose and clearest of styles, classified myths on death's origin into four types, viz., (i) The two messengers, (ii) The waxing and waning moon, (iii) The serpent and his cast skin, (iv) The banana tree (1913: 60). The first was common in parts of Africa and told how God sent some animal messenger, a chameleon say, to tell man that he would not die. Later God also sent another messenger, a lizard perhaps, to say that man would die. Unfortunately the chameleon was slow, lingered, ate and slept so that the lizard arrived first. That is why people now die, and why some hate the chameleon for being slow and some hate the lizard for being so quick. The second type offers some story in which people were originally like the moon; they died and came to life again, but some error caused them to lose this ability, leaving only the moon to wax and wane repeatedly. Often people had slept for three days between their lives, fixing upon three days as 'the interval between the disappearance and the reappearance of the new moon'. The third type is expressed in a Melanesian myth in which the Good Spirit loved people but hated serpents. He sent a messenger to tell humans to shed their skins like snakes and live for ever and to command snakes to die. The messenger blundered and did the opposite and that is why snakes shed their skins and men die. Frazer's final type – The banana tree – is represented in tales in which humanity asks God for something other than he has been giving them. In a Celebes form God lets down a stone on a rope instead of the usual pleasant fare. Humans object and God next lets down a banana which they readily receive. But God then tells them that they will be like bananas, the parent plant of which dies when it has produced fruit. Frazer acknowledges that some other myths do not fall into these categories as tales of places where, when people died, they were buried under a particular tree that brought them back to life again. So full did the world become that even the lizard could not walk freely. He suggested to the gravediggers that they bury people elsewhere; when they did so, mankind began to die and space became available once more. Other myths take the form of practical jokes or result from excessive curiosity or failing to observe commands or wise advice, and Frazer fills three volumes with such mythical reflections from pre-literate peoples. For him, this attention to death was aligned with the development of religion. Despite his polite, politically astute, and cautionary words Frazer thought that, 'as a partial explanation . . . of belief in gods . . . it is unquestionably true' that worship of gods emerged from the respectful attention initially paid to dead people. Frazer thought that people developed a belief in an afterlife because of their experience of the dead through dreams. The dead seem so 'alive' in dreams that they must exist somewhere. This prompted respectful and even worshipful attitudes to the deceased: the greater their status while alive the greater when dead. This doctrine or idea is called Euhemerism after Euhemerus, a fourth-century BCE Greek who thought that beliefs about the gods developed from tales concerning historical individuals.

Whether or not that kind of memory played any role in the evolution of religion, it remains the case that many people value themselves because of the past, including dead people, and because of the memory they themselves may leave behind when they die. This we have already seen in the ancient myth of Gilgamesh and the Netherworld, where the strength of identity of the dead in the afterlife depends upon their being remembered through funeral offerings, statues and the pronunciation of their names made by descendants in the land of the living. The man with no heir eats hard-baked brick-like bread while the man with seven sons sits on a throne as a kind of minor deity: by complete contrast the eunuch is just like a useless stick propped up against the wall (George 1999: 188). Not only are the dead maintained through the memory of the living but even their form of death influences their afterlife, with those having lost some body-part retaining that loss: the leper is set apart and the one who has lost a limb continues to lament the fact. Even the issue of cremation is raised, for the man who had been burnt to death, presumably accidentally, is not seen in the after-life: 'his ghost was not there, his smoke went up to the heavens'. A remarkable exception concerns stillborn babies who had never had names of their own and yet 'play amid syrup and ghee at tables of silver and gold' (George 1999: 189). Still, for the rest, even for one such as Gilgamesh, half divine and half human as he was, death is as certain as birth and comes as the darkest of days, as a flood and as a battle that cannot be won. Despite the fact that the afterlife is as an inescapable net, it should be faced not with remorse but openly.

In the world of the Americas, too, mythology explained the nature of death and the basis for ongoing human life on earth and hereafter, as with the Aztecs who were, in effect, the last of a long line of civilizations in meso-America prior to the sixteenth-century Spanish conquest. In Aztec myth contemporary men and women were born of the ground-up bones of earlier ancestors mixed with the blood of Quetzalcoatl who had journeyed to the underworld to collect these relics. This was celebrated in the annual feast to the dead and linked with fire-myths as the medium through which other mythical culture heroes had helped forge the universe itself. Such rites had their place in the *Templo Mayor*, the magnificent and enormous temple in the Aztec capital, now beneath Mexico City, and were probably practised long before it was built, just as dynamic and highly decorative rites are still performed in the 'Day of the Dead' festivities in today's Mexican cemeteries (Carmichael and Sayer 1991).

Such myth and ritual present death as a challenge to the living and, while assuming an afterlife, it is neither praised nor desired. Prime concern lies with relationships of friendship and kinship, bonds that make existence worth while and continue to give life meaning by fostering hope: hope that is intrinsic to the history of death, as shown in the previous chapter.


## The Dynamics of Memorial Sites

Hope enshrines the human desire to survive and flourish, a desire whose character is accentuated through confrontation with the negative features of death. With this in mind we now consider three ideal-type descriptions of both hope and memorial set up as sociological ideal types – abstract, descriptive cameos pinpointing the essential features of these topics. The three forms of hope are 'eternal', 'internal', and 'natural' and the three places are churchyard burials, private places for cremated remains and woodland burials or green funerals. Each type of hope is related to each type of place.

## Locating Hope: the Dynamics of Memorial Sites

To talk of 'locating hope' is to link place and feeling, location and sentiment. It brings together a combination of psychology–philosophy–theology on the one hand and geography and architecture on the other. This link exemplifies what Lindsay Jones in his intriguing study *The Hermeneutics of Sacred Architecture* describes in two ways as the ritual-architectural event and the ritual-architectural allurement of particular places (Jones 2000: 39–41, 75–79). Special places not only set an architectural framework around the hopes, fears and expectations that people bring to the ritual events taking place in them but they also draw and attract participants. Such places become built into not just our visual sense but also our spatial sense which, as Judith Okely argued, is 'greater than just the sense of sight: it extends to bodily memory and total ambience', and is something 'that cannot be reduced to words alone' (Okely, 1994: 60). So it is that many psychological experiences occur in specific places and enter into the memory and the identity of people. These are not simply places of memory, for memory as such is too single dimensional a notion to cope with the emotional and cultural complexity of dying, death and grief, but are also specially designated places possessing an allurement due to their historical–cultural past.

Such would have been the case for Egypt's ancient pyramid tombs as for today's Westminster Abbey in London in which many of the nation's most famed people are buried or memorialized. At the local level, too, many churches frame the local dead. When times change, through altered circumstance, dramatic events and the innovative creativity of individuals, new opportunities for allurement arise. In sociological terms new kinds of affinity develop between people and forms of memorial and hope.

## Place and Hope

In Bronislaw Malinowski's classic reflection on the anthropology of death, he emphasized the 'complex, double-edged play of hope and fear which sets in always in the face of death' (1974: 51). For him the 'desire for life' lay beneath all beliefs in immortality and religion. Working in the earlier decades of the twentieth century, his evolutionary and biological perspective saw humanity as set to survive by choosing life and adopting a positive view of existence even in the face of death. His adaptive view of religion lies close to Zygmunt Bauman's more recent discussion of mortality and immortality in which society is described as hiding death from its members lest they lose the will to live and thereby deny society its impetus to well-being (Bauman 1992).

Malinowski forcefully acknowledged the potentially disintegrating aspects of grief, especially in small, close-knit communities. For him funerary ritual, indeed religion itself, exists to 'reintegrate the group's shaken solidarity' and 're-establish its morale' (Malinowski 1974: 53). 'Hope over fear', that is Malinowski's formula for funerary ritual and, within his discussion, especially the crucial essay, 'Baloma: the spirits of the dead in the Trobriand Islands', location is all-important, for the spirit for the 'baloma' journeys to 'Tuma, a small island lying some ten miles to the northwest of the Trobriands' (1974: 150). Here we stress this geographical specificity within the extensive Trobriand mythology because it is reflected in many parts of the world, not least in the Christian reference to heaven and the Islamic hope of paradise.

Hope and place are inextricably aligned. Indeed, we could express this in question form and ask if hope is possible without place. If hope is not physically fashioned, can it exist? While, at first glance, this question seems to be entirely philosophical or, perhaps, theological, on further consideration it also begs an environmental response. My hypothesis is that hope is often contextual and that geography and architecture are vital for its flourishing. Hope is related to lived architectural events and to the allurement of place. Hope in Malinowski's Trobriand studies was aligned with the island of the dead; they had somewhere to go, but what of the dead in today's world?

## How to Speak of the Dead?

Most societies have, traditionally, 'located' their dead. The Christian dead are said to be in purgatory, in heaven, with Jesus or even asleep. Their bodies rest in peace in churchyard 'dormitories' and await the rising bell, or rather trumpet, of the last day. Such graves, whether in churchyards or cemeteries, emphasize this sense of the 'located' dead. Even 'burial at sea' 'located' the dead in that scripture dictated that, one day, the sea would also 'give up her dead'. How different this is from Zygmunt Bauman's notion of a post-modern world in which nobody is in 'a state of rest', from which we might infer that no body can, ultimately, 'rest in peace' either in this world or any world to come (1998: 78). The Egyptian pyramids stood in firm contrast to this fragility of contemporary uncertainties. As guardians of religious truth they were the very media of death-conquest, housing the specially prepared bodies of the great and, ultimately, transporting them to become the stars and deities of the heavens. It is against the background of such variation in human views of life and death that I now outline one scheme for interpreting both contemporary forms of hope and the memorials expressing that vital optimism. This scheme pairs 'location' and 'hope' in three sets.

## Location 1: Graveyard and Cemetery

Traditionally, the geography of village, town and city included a resting-place for the dead that mirrored the theology of hope provided by religion. Even the new cemeteries of urban nineteenth-century societies that demonstrated civic notions of urban planning also reflected religious identities that might include, for example, Catholic or Jewish sectors of cemeteries. The status of the living has also been reflected in the architectural location of their corpses. The metropolis was reflected in its necropolis, with the rich possessing extensive statues and the poor marked by simple graves or even massed in group burials devoid of individual recognition. Hope, in this sense, is not just some attitude towards an afterlife but also reflects the drive to survive and flourish in this life too. Still, the architecture of graves fostered a degree of hope both in words and symbol and, in the history of Christianity, 'the construction of funerary buildings was the first architectural activity of the early church', with St Peter's Rome beginning life as a covered cemetery (Turner 1979: 166). As Christianity's status became increasingly assured, so were the dead brought in from outside the city.

## Hope 1: Eternal, Eschatological Form of Identity

Theologically, traditional Christianity argued that the destiny of human beings lay in a divine future, in the afterlife. Individuals only came to fulfilment through what theologians call the last things of resurrection and judgement, heaven and hell. Because these are often described as eschatological events, as pertaining to the last times, we can argue for what I call the eschatological fulfilment of human identity. Hope is integral to this, as reflected in the traditional Christian burial sentences that we bury in 'sure and certain hope of the resurrection'. The grave is symbolic of Christ's grave and the Christian dead, like him, will rise again and in their new life will have a fullness hitherto unknown. Then they will know 'face to face' and not through 'a glass darkly' as St Paul expressed it. As Jon Davies insightfully observed, Christ's tomb marked the new territory of a new religion (1999: 8). Accordingly, the graveyards of Christendom have stood as markers for the hoped-for Kingdom of God. Sometimes, however, it has been human kingdoms that have come to sharp focus in memorials for the dead. This was especially true after the First World War, and to a degree after the Second World War in which many millions died. Throughout Europe war cemeteries were constructed and are, very largely, well maintained to this very day. Indeed these cemeteries, at the sites of major battles, have become much visited by family and friends of soldiers buried there or lost in battle. In practically every city, town, village and hamlet, and even in specific workplaces as, for example, in some major British shops and at colleges and universities, memorials were erected. Those named on them are not only recalled by their inscribed names but, in many British contexts, become the focus of memorial through the Remembrance Day rites in November. Today's ritual maintains and generates afresh a sense of time and history. Indeed, 'the generation of time' – in the double sense of both creating it and marking it for previous generations by present generations – stands as one major function of remembrance ritual. Jon Davies's research on war memorials of the recent European wars led him to the view that they expressed a view of death as a militaristic and heroic form of martyrdom and that this resulted in a kind of 'Euro-Christianity' whose ethic is one of sacrificial duty (Davies 1995). Jay Winter's historically and humanly sensitive study of the ways in which the First World War was commemorated stresses their importance in firmly fixing death within the grief of the bereaved, both individual and collective, and as he rightly says, 'the ways they did so have never been fully documented' (1995: 79). Despite the challenge of bringing any intelligibility to periods of human cruelty and warfare, certain major national memorial sites, such as the Cenotaph in Whitehall or Westminster Abbey in London, or Arlington National Cemetery in the USA, provide a focus for ritual that can embrace millions through television. Participation in ritual events, directly or even at a distance, can go some way in acknowledging the depth of chaos set against the human drive for meaning. Ritual action often yields a resolution of its own which rational discourse cannot match.

Apart from war, the deaths of daily life result in local church graveyards and civic cemeteries with their own forms of memorial. Many graves reflect the status of the dead through their degree of elaborateness or simplicity of structure; the kinship relationships of the dead are given with their dates of birth and death and, frequently, with some biblical text that reveals a degree of religious piety. Variations manifest the particular views of religious minorities. In the eighteenth century the Quakers, for example, initially did not allow the ostentation of headstones for graves and, with time, only moved to small stone markers bearing a minimum of information. This was a cultural expression of their idea of simplicity of life, a style they also sought to achieve in both dress and speech.

## Location 2: Cremation and Remains

While the advent of cremation in western society, as detailed in chapter 3, largely continued traditional Christian symbolism, it also opened up some quite new possibilities. Crematoria were often – but not always – designed with echoes of ecclesiastical buildings so that the built-architectural event of cremation echoed that of burial forms of funeral service. Ashes could be buried in graves along with coffins, in mini-graves of their own or could be strewn in gardens of remembrance at crematoria or in churchyards. In those ways cremated remains benefited from the pre-existing location of buried bodies or from the architecture of crematoria and their memorial gardens. Columbaria, special buildings with niches or shelves for the urns containing cremated remains, also furnished concrete architectural events with a strong classical antecedent.

But, with time and changing social values, cremation opened the possibility of privatizing cremated remains. Such remains were much more open to symbolic creativity than were dead bodies – for people can do more with ashes than with corpses. In fact it took until the mid-1970s for Britons to begin taking cremated remains away from crematoria and engaging in private rites, locating remains in a wide variety of personally chosen spots, often related to the interests, hobbies, or to the relationship of the dead. Here was a new invention of tradition: people did novel things with material of a high symbolic value and did so quite apart from the formal rites and control of church or state. Similarly, the design of crematoria began to alter, with a decrease in Christian symbolism or the possibility for the provision of many forms of religious or no-religious expression. The nature of architectural allurement was shifting. And this at a time when a large minority of Britons did not believe in life after death and, even if they did, they seldom tied it to traditional ideas of resurrection.

In the USA, American English developed the word 'cremains' as an abbreviation of 'cremated remains'. This is an interesting word in that it removes 'cremation' from immediate reference and might be said to marginalize the very element that yields the product. This, however, is not strange for in many US contexts the actual crematorium may be quite separate from where the funeral service takes place. Yet, at the same time, the word slightly transforms 'remains' to make them something special; one might say that it customizes the product. Something of this slight confusion is reflected in one American best-seller novel:

'Actually, it's kind of funny – they don't call them *remains*: they call them "cremains". But we still think the ashes might be coming' (Eggers 2000: 223).

## Hope 2: Internal, the Retrospective Fulfilment of Identity

The new rites of privatization of cremated remains may well reflect that pattern of belief or absence of belief. The hope involved in changed rites can also be interpreted as a reversal of the traditional Christian notion of hope lying in the eschatological fulfilment of identity, with its possible idea of lovers meeting again in heaven for some eternal family future as discussed earlier in this book. So it is that an eschatological fulfilment is replaced by a retrospective fulfilment of identity of both the dead and of the bereaved partner.

Relatives take cremated remains and place them in locations of high personal significance for the deceased person or for their relationship with that person. Throughout most of the twentieth century these remains had been buried or scattered at crematoria where special gardens of remembrance were constructed. A relatively small number were placed in various forms of decorative urns for permanent retention in columbaria: the columbarium being a modern redevelopment of the classic Roman niched wall building for remains, itself named after the dovecote with its individual compartments. But, now the dynamics of memorial sites shift; they no longer benefit from this public frame of significance. Private, personal, even idiosyncratic factors replace established cultural ideas. This suggests that 'hope', too, shifts in significance. Fond memory replaces hope. Ashes are not deposited in sure and certain hope of the resurrection but in deep memory and engagement with the past. Here the identity of the living frames the location of the dead. The significance of the ashes and of their location will hold only as long as the living survive. Devoid of the wider public architecture, memory becomes less durable than does publicly framed hope. But, and this is perhaps the crucial fact, given that personal wishes are paramount in a privatized consumerist culture, it is what the relative wants that counts.

Here I would add that whether in public cemetery or privately located remains it is wise to note that the bereaved still visit and talk to the dead, they activate their memories and selectively draw from them as they will. In this they are free to locate and manipulate hope as a positive sentiment within their own life. This brings to focus the fact that death is a relational factor as far as the living are concerned. The extent to which that relationship is a basis for hope now becomes the crucial issue. When memory is excited within pre-existing locations of religious or civic hope it may be expected to share in the public fund of memory, at least to some extent, but that cannot be guaranteed with private sites. Cremated remains, in other cultural contexts, can foster the memory of the dead, as in India where Mahatma Ghandi's remains were divided and sent to different parts of the country, allowing different regions a sense of participation in the memorial of that great leader. Historically speaking, there were similar cases of parts of bodies being buried in different places, as with David Livingstone's heart being buried in Africa while his body was returned to England.

Today, the individual choice of the bereaved as a consumer of ritual services becomes important but with the result that cultural clashes may arise between the guardians of architectural-ritual sites and their users. When, for example, a Church of England dignitary does not allow a churchyard gravestone to carry the word 'Dad', regarding it as somewhat vulgar, he is viewed as insensitive to the needs of the bereaved. Within a consumerist culture, grief, like style, can be viewed as an individual choice that should be treated respectfully by those providing services. Differences of opinion can become problematic if, for example, church officials see themselves as, primarily, representing historical and traditional religion with a responsibility for social architecture of death and not simply as providers of an arena in which individuals are free to do as they wish. Because our society has become highly sensitized to death, as to human rights in general, it becomes increasingly unacceptable to set individual needs against the potential values of wider society.

The bridge between society and individual is always many-spanned. Some scholars approach the history of humanity with the idea that people in one era are really quite different from those in another. Doubtless, there is much truth in the fact that our culture forms much of us in its own image but, even so, this should not compel us to assume radical differences over certain emotions and moods. Indeed, I suspect that aspects of, for example, fear and grief, as of love, hate and excitement, are undercurrents of common human experience that endure over millennia. Judicious and charitable caution must be exercised over changing times and places.

We might, for example, take the case of tears. As an expression of grief, tears are far from simple, running, as they do, the spectrum from inner privacy to public display. Durkheim's sociological eye saw in tears a message to the community from the bereaved, a social expectation and duty. And there are times when people must be seen to weep; anything else would be disrespectful and throw into doubt their relationships with the dead. But there are also times when weeping is private, of the heart and for the heart, as is inevitable given the depth and complexity of human relationships. There are some tears that would not make social sense and come into their own only in private. Even the provision of paid public wailers does not presume lack of personal loss on the part of their patron. William Blake's expression, 'For a Tear is an intellectual thing', marks a poetic defence against any sharp division between reason and feeling, and clearly affirms how ideas may well take the form of emotion; his is a reminder of the complexity of life (Blake 1874: 159).

## Location 3: Woodland Burial

My third ideal type of funeral location develops what we have already discussed in chapter 4 in terms of ecological thought and woodland burial. In a variety of contexts across the United Kingdom some local authorities and private individuals are making provision for those who wish to be buried neither in graveyards nor cemeteries but in what is best described as natural surroundings. Here we move beyond the architectural frame to the allurement of nature. The very concept of 'nature' is, of course, itself cultural and means different things within different societies, just as the 'countryside' carries different connotations as between England and France. It is interesting, for example, to see how Philippe Ariès sees death as one of the powerpoints of 'nature' against which culture had not been entirely successful in establishing a defence (1991: 393). Still, studies of the iconography of landscape, especially by geographers, have done much to show the cultural values vested in particular forms of forest, woodland and landscaped gardens, though much remains to be done in extending such work into death studies (Cosgrove and Daniels 1988). Ultimately, 'nature' is anything but natural in the strict sense, being inseparable from changing cultural values.

Alfred Gell was right, I think, in his view that 'the geographers' maps have profound but unexplored implications for the process of human cognition' within that 'choreography' of daily life that brings many a constraint to our movement (1992: 321). Graveyards and cemeteries along with traditional crematoria are marked on maps and present just such constraints upon how we relate to our dead and to our own post-mortem location. However, cremated remains reduced what Gell called 'capability constraints', the limit of only being in one place at one time, since ashes could be divided and be in many places at once. Such a degree of freedom might be seen as appropriate for a post-modern self and fostered in the many choices outlined by such sources as *The New Natural Death Handbook* (Albery et al. 1997). Included in this approach to space is a shift of views on such things as coffins and funeral directors. The pursuit of 'natural' funerals is often aligned with new forms of containers for the body in the form of shrouds, body carriers, cardboard coffins or in coffins that might foster early decay and return of the body to the earth. Indeed some, like the American ecological pagan Edward Abbey, conceive 'authentic death' as involving being 'eaten by other living entities' (Taylor, B. 1995: 107). Less dramatically, but equally sincerely, some family members want to be more involved with the entire event, from preparation of the body to the ritual form itself.

## Hope 3: Natural, the Ecological Fulfilment of Identity

Here ideas of simplicity replace cultural elaboration. The emphasis falls upon actual bodies and their return to the earth in a way that cannot be equated with the traditional Christian liturgical phrase 'earth to earth, ashes to ashes, dust to dust'. That formula came invested with the mythology of Eden, of the fall, and of the tragic destiny of humanity disobedient to God. Ecology presents us with a different mythology. And here I use the word mythology to refer to constructed cultural stories filling accounts of the meaning of life with particular moral values. For here we are engaged primarily neither with the eschatological nor the retrospective fulfilment of identity but with an ecological fulfilment, one that may, however, link a former way of life with a hoped-for future. One major factor that has come to influence life in many societies in recent decades is the issue of ecology as a scientifically informed moral theory of the world. This complex issue, already addressed in chapter 4, suggests that the corpse is viewed not as the symbolic corpse of Adam and Eve, the sinful pair punished by death for eating of the forbidden tree, but of a responsible human being aware of the world of which he or she was a part and of which he or she now continues as a biological complement, motivated by an intellectual ethic of identity. These people choose to be of the earth; they are not compelled to be dust to dust.

## Memorial Texts

Time alone will tell how woodland burial may furnish distinctive sites of long-term significance and affect the public face of human experience. The great cemeteries of the nineteenth century provided an important public record of death, of the sentiments of people as well as of their status and social standing. The advent of cremation changed this historical stratum of recognition, especially once the relatively short-lived influence of columbaria and concrete markers of cremated remains gave way to the private disposal of remains. Some historically minded observers often comment on the consequential outcome of the apparent disappearance of the dead from the archaeological record. The creation of crematorium books of remembrance, and now of their computerized equivalents, goes some way in marking the departed but these are of a different order from gravestones ever-present in public cemeteries.

Memorial books came into existence, largely in the mid-twentieth century, because it was easy for cremated remains and their location to be unrecorded or to be simply an impersonal grid-reference upon a site map. For those whose cremated remains are taken away from a crematorium and scattered in some location such as a mountain or river, the need for a fixed reference point may be all the greater. These books are made and inscribed with great care; some even follow the methods of medieval monks in making velum parchment and illuminating the name or some added illustration with considerable artistry. Kept in glass cases at crematoria, the page with the date of cremation is turned each day so that visiting relatives can mark anniversaries. Families may purchase copies of their own book-entry to keep at home, allowing domestic life to echo the more formal location of the crematorium. An even more common form of memorializing the dead is that of newspaper memorial and obituary columns. From local to national publications, these note the passing of individuals, with the more famous having their life-achievements recalled. Such obituaries can, themselves, provide an interesting insight into the way attitudes to death change over time and place.

## The National Memorial Arboretum

That public aspect of memorial is reflected in numerous ways in contemporary societies, for not everything is privatized. The close of the twentieth and opening decade of the twenty-first century, for example, witnessed one particular British burial place and site of memorializing the dead that has emerged in relation to 'nature', though not entirely for 'ecological' reasons. The National Memorial Arboretum located near Alrewas in Staffordshire and opened by The Duchess of Kent in May 2001 was the outcome of an idea of David Childs who conceived the idea during a visit to the USA's Arlington National Cemetery. He wanted somewhere to commemorate the generation of Britons and others – perhaps some eighty million in all – who had engaged in the Second World War and other twentieth-century fields of battle, who had raised memorials to the war dead without having their own, often civilian, bravery commemorated. With financial support from a variety of sources the woodland began to be planted in 1997, partly in relation to the newly encouraged National Forest that was being planted across England. Plots have been set aside to commemorate specific groups as well as individuals. Part of the emphasis of this and similar woodland ventures lies on the nature of growth itself: and here trees are remarkably suitable objects whose symbolic power can hardly be overlooked. For many cultures, there is that about trees which speaks of a powerful sense of life that endures beyond a single generation and which may last for centuries. The cultural image of the yew tree in British churchyards already affords a deep conceptual resource for new tree planting. Indeed, the National Memorial Arboretum included the planting of a 'Millennium Yew'. The whole venture of planning, patronage and dedication included politicians, church leaders and military figures and shows how such a memorial site can muster key social personnel.

## Lifestyle – Death-Style

Changing possibilities over memorializing the dead within contemporary society inevitably raise problems between the theological words of church liturgies and the private beliefs and values of individuals. The later twentieth and the early twenty-first century is a period in which the role of official religion in relation to individual life has undergone dramatic changes. Historically, churches have played an absolutely central role in the rites of death in practically every Christian-influenced culture. As increasing numbers of people no longer believe in traditional ideas of resurrection and heavenly life, and as churches no longer hold a place of unquestioned influence in society at large, it is to be expected that individuals whose lives are increasingly grounded in ideas of personal choice should extend that choice from simple commodities to the welfare realms of life and death. Set within increasingly market-led, consumerist, societies embraced by an even wider culture committed to human rights, it is perhaps inevitable that people's concern over their individual lifestyle should also extend to their death-style. What is at stake in these changes is the ability of 'service providers' not only to provide a variety of forms of disposal but also to foster the hope that has vitalized human approaches to death throughout history.

Whether through gravestones, remains cast to the winds or through woodland burial we find human beings relating to their dead. For some, memory's emphasis is grounded in an external place, for others in a deeply rooted memory. Recall may come through music, a photograph or the ongoing family likeness in children and grandchildren. Being the embodied creatures we are, the 'place' of memory may be none other than ourselves. 'I am very like my father', says an elderly man reviewing his own life and yet being unable to do so without picturing his long-dead father's way of doing something. Only he knows how handwriting binds him to his past and allows the past to live on with immediate effect in a relatively placeless act of memory.

# Chapter 7

# Fear of Death

The spectrum of the fear of death is many-coloured. Some see it as so black that it dominates all other human emotions, while for others it pales into such relative insignificance that it passes into an anticipated excitement. This chapter explores several of these shades of meaning, beginning with mythical and theological ideas before considering the all too practical onslaught of sickness and plague and ending with wider psychological and philosophical themes.

Specific fears take many forms, from fear of burial alive to the anticipated torment of a hellish after-world: from deep anxiety of leaving one's family to fend for themselves to the dread of personal extinction. The imaginations of some societies are also haunted, often by the fear of those already 'dead' but still reckoned to be a threat to the living, whether as judgemental ancestors or as ghosts, as vampires or zombies. However, although widespread, such fears are not universal, with much depending upon context and the moral webs of relationship, of sense of achievement and fulfilment and of belief in human destiny.

## A Mythical Form

Once again the myth of Gilgamesh is instructive, this time in revealing an early human account of the fear of death. In chapter 2 we saw this ancient Babylonian material describe how Gilgamesh experienced the death of Enkidu – his dear friend and companion in hardship. When Gilgamesh recognizes that he, too, will die he tells how sorrow has entered his heart, making him wander in the wild, in the very environment out of which Enkidu had emerged. Here, in one of the earliest written human statements of the bare fact of mortality, Gilgamesh clearly states, 'I am afraid of death' (George 1999: 70). Interestingly, the text tells how his grief is partly assuaged when, after sleep, he awakes and with a sense of the power conferred by the moon as the very lamp of the gods, he 'grew glad of life'. In his new-found strength he kills lions, eats their flesh and digs wells and drinks their waters, dramatically reflecting an earlier episode when Enkidu exhorted him to 'forget death and seek life'. Nevertheless, his fear of death, triggered by his beloved friend's death, only grows worse as he ponders his own mortality and seeks a cure for it before, finally, becoming resigned to its inevitability. Still, his wisdom grows through his grief, as does his ultimate adaptation to the finality framed by his acceptance of mortality. This myth alerts us to the fact that the deeply human 'flight or fight response' is not the only form of human reaction to contexts of fear.

## Hinduism, Buddhism

Wisdom, in this sense of an insightful acceptance of life, has developed in several directions within the major religious traditions of humanity, not least in Hinduism and Buddhism.

Hinduism coped with death not only through its notion of *karma* as the ultimate moral process undergirding transmigration and reincarnation but also through the idea of *ashrama* or stages of life by which an individual passes from being a student to a householder, then from beginning to withdraw from social duties to a final withdrawal from all social obligations in preparation for death and the soul's transmigration to another life. While this social acknowledgement of existence in its varied phases contextualizes the fear of death socially and domestically, it does not mean to say that individuals do not fear death. It is not accidental, for example, that one of the founding stories of Buddhism's emergence tells how the young Hindu, Gautama, encountered the bitterness of life by seeing a corpse and was launched on the search for enlightenment. In its more philosophically grounded practice Buddhism made a major attempt to engage with the meaning of life and death by arguing that all of death's apparent reality is as deceptive as are fears themselves, or even as the sense of a distinct individual identity. Although this radical approach with its embedded monastic way of life has generally come to exist alongside a multiplicity of folk-beliefs that detracts from its prime focus, there is much in Buddhist thought that appeals strongly to increasing numbers in today's world where many desire a spirituality devoid of traditional Christian orthodoxy.

## Christianity

As far as that Christian orthodoxy is concerned it consists, very largely, in an assault upon the fear of death. In St Paul's major exposition of Christianity death is described as 'the last enemy to be destroyed' (1 Corinthians 15: 26). For him, and for millions since, that triumph was rooted in resurrection and the hope of life beyond death. Many subsequent Christian thinkers have explored death's dominance in a variety of ways and here we focus on several of the more significant and recent contributions.

In the mid-nineteenth century Søren Kierkegaard took up the issue of death and hope as part of his extensive analysis *The Sickness unto Death* ([1849]1968). His complex description focused on the nature of despair as the 'sickness unto death' and is important for both the history of existential philosophy and for Christian spirituality because of the way it explores the nature of hope. Kierkegaard does this by excavating the depths of individuals and of the 'self' that he thinks we should give our all to become and which so very few actually achieve. In some ways his formulation predates Freud's interest in the unconscious and sets the scene for later approaches to the central topic of identity and of the many psychological, social and religious dynamics that surround an individual on the road to gaining a sense of self. Kierkegaard constructs sets of cameos, detailed descriptions of how people think and experience their emotions and sense of self in terms of hope and despair, and death is far from the terror one might expect it to be. For him the profounder sadness in human life lies not in death but in the failure of many people to encounter all that detracts from true personhood, a failure to truly become themselves. For him there is a fate worse than death: it is not to become 'ourselves'.

## Albert Schweitzer and C. S. Lewis

One of the greatest Christians of the early twentieth century, Albert Schweitzer (1875–1957), also addressed himself to death in a most telling way in the form of a sermon delivered in 1907. It is worth dwelling on this creative piece because it pinpoints so many themes that would be developed by others as the twentieth century advanced. Telling how all things are subjected to death, he begins, rather like Sigmund Freud, by aligning death with the decay of nature but, unlike Freud, Schweitzer goes on to address death as a theological problem. Death, like the transience of so many things, exists all around us but, he asks, does it not also reign within us? For him the terror and fear of death had long been used within Christianity to 'frighten men into believing in eternal life'. And the result of that, he reckons, was – 'Numbness, numbness'. Because such a fear-motivation had been so often repeated it had, he believed, lost its effect and led to a 'conspiracy of silence' in a kind of comedy that pretends death does not exist: but the comedy only generates a loneliness in the players. He gives what might be regarded as an early appreciation of a popular medicalization of death, describing how mourners will stand around discussing the deceased's sickness, the length of his illness, who his doctor was, and of what sickness he died.

But Schweitzer advocated a different approach. Though he knows it is not strictly orthodox, he believed that we should develop a 'calm and natural' approach to death, one he believed was inspired by the Christian faith. This outlook realistically acknowledges how dreadful it would be to be caught up in earthly life without end. This perspective begins to breed a 'true love for life' which accepts each day 'as a gift' and 'creates an inward freedom from material things'. Even if this state is attained one fear remains and it is the fear of 'being torn' from those who need us. For Schweitzer the deepest meaning in life comes from the sense of what others need from him and he from them. Here he speaks the language of attachment and detachment, one that the psychologists would pursue in their theories of grief as chapter 2 showed. Ultimately he sees his own Christian interpretation of 'overcoming death' as lying not in an ignoring of death but in the acceptance of life as a daily gift. This he sees as expressing the biblical idea of sharing in Christ's death and resurrection. He, finally, adds a note on 'immortality' to say that it is a word used too easily to comfort those who are dying, and becomes superficial when so used. Schweitzer's emphasis is upon eternal life as a 'present experience' that 'cannot be described in words' and which may not be in conformity with 'the traditional picture of it'. He concludes that 'something within us does not pass away' but lives and works 'wherever the kingdom of the spirit is present'.

A much more orthodox near-contemporary of Schweitzer, C. S. Lewis (1893–1963), in his influential and popular book on *Miracles*, also draws attention to the fear of death as a topic 'implicit in nearly all private conversations on the subject, and in much modern thought about the survival of the human species' (1947: 151). He was, of course, writing at the end of the Second World War when millions more had been added to the list of those who died untimely deaths. He contrasted this 'natural' attitude of fear both with the Stoic view that death 'doesn't matter' and should be treated as a matter of indifference, and with his own very traditional Christian interpretation of death as both the outcome of human rebellion against God and as the medium through which God saves humanity through the resurrection of Jesus Christ. In a strange comment Lewis suggests that 'almost the whole of Christian theology could perhaps be deduced from the two facts that (a) That men make course jokes, and (b) That they "feel the dead to be uncanny"' (1947: 154). While hardly an accurate route to theology's core, these comments elaborate Lewis's conviction that human beings sensed, in jokes, that they were rather funny animals and, in death, that their real inward unity had come apart. People sensed that they should exist as a profound unity of spirit and body: indeed, he believed that they had been created as such and it was only in the Fallen state that they now parted from each other at death. Accordingly, both the corpse and the ghost – as the manifestation of spirit apart from the body – are 'detestable'. On this count the fear of death results from an acknowledgement that we become something that we ought not to be and we lose ourselves. For Lewis, as a Christian thinker and popular apologist, this point of loss also becomes the pivotal point of salvation at which Christ, having descended from heaven into the depths of hellish death, resurfaces in resurrection to guarantee a reuniting of spirit and body in the future resurrection of believers.

Lewis's belief in heaven is strongly orthodox and he speaks of it in several of his books as a state that will appear more real than even life on earth. In our final chapter we return to both Lewis and Schweitzer to address the issue of what death may mean for some today.

## Essential Fear

Quite apart from theological arguments, fear is a general human emotion grounded in the fact that, as self-conscious beings, we are aware that we live in a dangerous world where other people, animals, plants and the physical environment can all do us harm, injure or kill us. A deep sense of attention to danger lies at the core of survival. Intelligence of various sorts, intellectual, emotional and relational, alerts us to these potential dangers and prepares modes of avoidance and defence. While fear of the dark may be considered irrational in some contemporary, suburban homes or in landscape largely devoid of poisonous flora and fauna, it is far from irrational in unlit city side-streets, let alone in forest contexts in countries where dangerous species flourish. Since fear has to do with the risks of survival, it is natural that fear and death should be close partners but not, as we have already intimated, that flight or fight should be the only responses to death.

## Plague

No brief history of death's enveloping of people would be acceptable without some account of past and present examples of nature's devastation of human society with the inevitable sense of fear they have evinced. The best-known case in Europe, that of the Plague, occurred between 1347 and 1350 in the form of a highly infectious illness spread by fleas. Originating somewhere in China in the 1330s, it was spread to the west by merchant seamen. Called the Bubonic Plague – from the word 'bubo' used to describe the swellings of the lymphatic nodes in groin and armpits – it knew no bounds, with the result that up to two-thirds of the population of some towns died. Some reckon that, in all, some twenty-five million Europeans died. The severe depopulation that followed was not reversed until the sixteen hundreds. One positive cultural effect was to increase the status of labourers and influence change in medieval society. These deaths involved a number of wider consequences which included both a decrease in dedication to religion on the one hand and an increase in piety towards some 'plague-saints' and shrines on the other. In terms of historical literature the Italian Giovanni Boccaccio (1313–75) wrote his *Decameron* as a description of events accounting for how the plague affected people, not least in terms of the decrease in respectful attitude to the dying and the dead when the living had to consider their own chances of survival by ensuring only minimal contact with the sick.

## Modern Devastations

Some five hundred years later, in the nineteenth century, cholera became a major killer in many European societies whose densely packed industrial towns and cities were largely devoid of proper sanitation and healthy water supplies, the latter being a key factor in the spread of the disease. Sweeping through communities, it triggered high levels of alarm and was, not infrequently, talked of as a plague and likened to the biblical plagues of Egypt (Exodus 7–11). Some religious groups even saw cholera as a fulfilment of biblical warnings concerning the last days. One Mormon leader, for example, writing from Wales in July 1849, observed that, 'this plague is more dreadful in places where the gospel has been most preached', implying that it fell on those who had not accepted the message (Davies 1987: 9).

In the twentieth century, at least two different illnesses also claimed significant numbers of lives. The 'Spanish Influenza', though largely lost to popular memory due to its striking in 1918–19, in the shadow of the devastation of the First World War, caused the death of some twenty million people in two years, 'more than died in the whole of the First World War' (Mims 1998: 21). The fear of death in terms of illness is, itself, strongly variable from culture to culture and age to age and few adults in Western societies would, for example, now fear dying of respiratory lung infections, tuberculosis or diarrhoea infections and yet, in the 1990s, these were accounting for approximately nearly ten million deaths each year, especially of children, in some less developed societies. Malaria probably adds another two million, with hepatitis B and measles a further million each. By contrast, the fear of cancer is real for many, even when some forms of the disease are becoming increasingly more treatable.

Towards the close of the twentieth century, however, considerable attention was drawn to the HIV virus, with its associated full-blown manifestation as AIDS. This echoed something of 'the plague' as it began to make a highly publicized impact, initially through the death of homosexual men in western societies, along with some drug users who shared contaminated hypodermic syringes. Even medically controlled blood transfusion was responsible for some infection. People who otherwise were healthy and successful and who might have anticipated relatively long life were being cut down in their prime. This, inevitably perhaps, attracted critical comment from some religious sources who saw AIDS as a kind of divine punishment for what they saw as immoral behaviour. However, with time, the virus became increasingly evident through heterosexual contacts, most especially in Third-World and some developing societies. Indeed, by the beginning of the twenty-first century it was assuming epidemic proportions in parts of Africa and beyond. Babies could be infected in the womb and, in countries with high birth-rates, many children were being left as orphans when the parents died young. In parts of Africa HIV–AIDS combined with tuberculosis in a deadly alliance. In some countries, due to the pressures of moral convention, authorities even resisted linking AIDS with sex or even denied its increasing prevalence, an attitude that frustrated potential programmes of education for protection. This combines with the relative expense of potentially helpful drugs so that, as the twenty-first century begins, the future demography of several African countries is unpredictable, as are the consequences of debilitating illness and early death upon their economic well-being.

## Philosophical Fears

From this fear of biologically rooted death we move to the human psyche, and to some philosophical reflections of human finitude. In much western writing, not least from the USA in the mid-twentieth century, the fear of death assumed a dominant though varied role. In part this came on the back of the world wars and the subsequent Cold War between 'the West' and Communism. In the 1950s the philosophical theologian Paul Tillich (1886–1965) said of his generation, 'We have become a generation of the End', (1973: 279). For him the complacency of the nineteenth and early twentieth centuries had had its 'lid torn off', with the picture of death returning as in the Middle Ages with its 'figure of Death . . . the Dance of death' reappearing in and through war, Holocaust and forced exile. Ironically, the anthropologist Geoffrey Gorer saw these death fears as being hidden rather than displayed. Indeed, he famously couched these attitudes to death in terms of pornography, with death having replaced sex as a topic avoided in ordinary life (1956). Here we witness an irony over the twentieth-century fear of death. The preacher advances it as a description of the human condition, the anthropologist describes it as a hidden force. One way of allowing each some credibility is to develop the topic of the 'fear of death' as a form of 'fear of life'.

Many philosophers, whether professional or, for example, as existentialist novelists, have seen that attitudes to death are closely related to our sense of identity, to the way we live and to the meaning we sense in the life we lead. With this in mind I would argue that fear of death is related to the fear of life. This fear of life is, itself, grounded in a multitude of fears, from war to plague and poverty. In particular, the fear of life is the ultimate fear of life's meaninglessness. Failure to face the fact that one's life is, at some level, senseless is the fear of life. This can involve the fear that one is not really loved by one's closest family and friends to the fear that one's life endeavours actually amount to nothing. Similarly, younger or middle-aged people, much caught up in many ventures, making plans for their work and for their growing family, may well fear death as that which cuts across their accustomed sense of being in control of life. While an old person may long to meet their deceased spouse in the afterlife, the successful executive and family man fears what might befall his wife and children in his absence. So, too, with many a mother whose fear is for her children more than for herself. The decline of religious belief, whether in a historical culture through some process of secularization or in an individual's own life, can also foster a questioned and doubted identity and lead to fear.

But care must be taken not to exaggerate this fear of life nor the fear of death. For there are some who, contrary to popular image, do not fall under its imperious control. These include those with large families and much to show for their life's work, as well as those suffering from terminal illness or simply much wearied by old age and possessing a sense of either awaiting an afterlife or of simply having come to the end of their life journey. A degree of welcome resignation to death is not uncommon amongst the very old. So, too, where religious traditions are strong and influential people often possess a high degree of awareness of the meaningfulness of the world and of their place in it, where a sense of identity leads to love of life and an acceptance of death, often with death being part of an ongoing scheme of identity. Some mention ought also to be made of those for whom death is anticipated as an end of the moral compromises and intractable mess of life. Albert Camus caught something of this in his novel dealing with such a moral 'plague' when he writes, 'some of us feel such a desperate weariness, a weariness from which nothing remains to set us free, except death' ([1947] 1960: 207).

## Psychology and Fear of Death

Some of these dynamics of fear of death can be developed further in terms of psychological studies of human identity.

Erik Erikson in the 1950s put these very well from his own psychological viewpoint that 'healthy children will not fear life if their elders have enough integrity not to fear death' (1965: 261). His notion of 'integrity' is particularly useful because it allows us to revisit what was said in our first chapter on identity, the human drive for meaning and the mutual relationship of life and death. Erikson saw integrity, or 'ego integrity' as he called it, as the opposite of despair. It involves a kind of cultural certainty in relation to the orderly meaningfulness of existence. It fully acknowledges the different interpretations of life given by other cultures and in other historical periods, yet, instead of lapsing into some sort of cultural relativity that breeds despair, it engenders an integrity of the self. It is precisely against this backcloth of identity that 'death loses its sting' while, conversely, the fear of death signifies the absence or loss of just such a sense of integrity (1965: 260). On the broadest canvas Erikson believed that those whose lives were grounded in a sense of trust of others and whose world had come to assume a degree of orderliness and meaningfulness would not approach death in fear or despair. There is a great deal of truth in Erikson's vision of how people grasp life and live it and share their endeavour with new generations. In his own psychological terms he gives shape to our more socio-logical view of 'transcendence' which accepts the flawed nature of life's negativities and interprets them to advantage. But, at the end of the day so much depends upon the individual, on each one of us and our own personal story of life experience, and it is with that in mind that we take an exaggerated example of the fear of death in the context of one very well-known artist.

## Picasso

A powerful example of the fear of death as an underlying influ-ence on life is found in Picasso. Though mentioned in chapter 5, we return to him here to highlight a distinctive pattern of fear of death in which a strongly creative individual is driven by his own narcissism to assert himself against the world at large, albeit always with the knowledge that he is mortal. He turns away from traditional religious belief in an afterlife, or at least is strongly ambivalent in his acceptance of it, and comes to be most vulner-able when confronted by death whilst driven by narcissism – that emotional fixation on self. This scene is made even more complex if we accept the theory that early grief helps foster adult charismatic personality in leaders of movements. From his earliest days Picasso felt a profound sense of being without equal, one who was to be loved and followed, even if he, himself, found it difficult to love others in return. In Picasso, a profound early grief, an immense charisma, a dramatic artistic creativity and a rejection of religious tradition, alongside an ongoing mag-ical sense of the consequence of his own 'magical' words and actions, combine to make death all the more problematic. How could such a one die? That sense of immortality that sometimes envelops adolescent life had expanded in the self that was full of human dynamism and a sense of potential that brooks no constraint. In such a life, death is doubly difficult to ponder and face when it befalls family and friends.

## Fears Real and Imagined

From this biographical sketch we move to wider realms of dread in which both real and imaginary death fears haunt the life of the living. The fear of being buried alive is one that displays with clarity the marks of time and place. It gained its name, taphophobia – fear of the grave – from the Italian psychiatrist E. Morselli in 1891, as documented by Jan Bondeson whose study entitled *Buried Alive* analyses the extensive literature that exists on premature burial (2001: 276). Bondeson shows how, for example, there was considerable medical debate in the eighteenth and nineteenth centuries on the accuracy of medically ascertaining death, especially in the light of periodic cases of those declared dead but who came to life again. He emphasizes the fact that the agreed-upon signs of death focused on the heartbeat, breathing, and a general sense of unconsciousness that had prevailed from antiquity until the seventeenth century. The possibility of people given to certain forms of fit and unconsciousness being mistakenly taken for dead and then buried alive could not be ignored, as in the case in Cologne of the famous philosopher Duns Scotus (1265–1308). Much later, in the early eighteenth century, some advocated the use of pins inserted in the toenails to ascertain death in questionable cases and pin examples have been found amongst the fifty thousand or so who died in the plague of Marseilles in the 1720s. Amongst the variety of funeral reformers emerging in the nineteenth century, including many who pressed for cremation, were anti-premature-burial campaigners such as The London Society for the Prevention of Premature Burial founded in 1896; some of these argued that as many as 10 per cent of the population were buried alive (Bondeson 2001: 278).

What, then, of contemporary fears in relation to death and disposal? In interviews with just over sixteen hundred English and Scots in 1995 my own research, for example, asked people if they possessed any fears or anxieties over burial on the one hand and cremation on the other. The great majority of people (81 per cent) reckoned to have none, but approximately 13 per cent said they did have concerns. While this is a relatively low percentage of the sample it would, as a representative sample of the public, still involve a large number of people in the nation at large where some 600,000 die each year. What was particularly interesting in our British research findings was that more people had worries over burial than over cremation. So, for example, nearly 300 people feared being buried alive, eaten by worms, rotting or simply being cold in the ground, while about 130 were afraid of being burnt, or burnt alive. The other major feature of these results concerned gender: women were three times as likely to express a fear than were men, and this was the same for burial fears as for cremation fears (Davies and Shaw 1995: 26–8). It is not easy to explain why there was such a difference between the sexes. I do not think it is because men were less free in expressing their feelings on these issues, as is often suggested to explain gender difference. It may, rather, be a question of identity, of how women and men picture themselves to themselves when they ponder their own sense of identity. Perhaps some women have been encouraged to think of themselves in terms of how they look, so that identity and an imagined physical image go together. On this basis the very thought of rotting implies a sense of loss of identity.

Still, for the great majority, fears of burial and cremation were of limited concern. If the twentieth century brought a reduction in fear through a greater degree of confidence in the medical diagnosis of death it also, by contrast, enhanced something of the older fears through new practices such as the harvesting of organs from those reckoned to be dead but kept biologically 'alive' until their surgical removal. Here distinctions between pragmatic fears of premature burial and the vaguer worries over death in general begin to merge into each other and are over-shadowed by further anxieties over the dead and their possible interaction with the living.

## Imaginative Fears

In the strictly more imaginative world of literature and its fur-ther publicity through cinema and television the fear of death has been fed by an entire genre of the 'living dead', replete with bloodsucking visions of vampires, not least with Count Dracula and his minions inhabiting the dusky corners of relatively ur-banized minds. The nineteenth century, in particular, took these elemental fears of nature and worked them into fancies and fantasies that helped provide a mythical form for the many ex-plorations of mood and sentiment of the Romantic period. As James Twitchell expressed it, 'The first vampire stories, Byron's "Fragment" and John Polidori's *The Vampyre* (1819), introduced the demon to the worn-out Gothic novel, and in three decades the vampire had become a stock character to be exploited with-out mercy in Thomas Pecket Prest's *Varney the Vampyre*' (1981: 6).

Behind the numerous films that would be made in the twen-tieth century lay both this literature and its background folklore, well known in Eastern Europe but reflected in very many soci-eties across the world, in which certain individuals are deemed abnormal and do not die as do other people. On the contrary, they return to disturb the living but, unlike troublesome ghosts, these revenants are irrevocably tied to their bodies – often be-lieved to emerge from their tomb at night – and take their toll on the bodies of the living.

The living-dead are associated with a great variety of potential causes of their condition. Perhaps they were born with some physical abnormality, had been radically anti-social in their life-time, were suicides or died abnormal deaths, or some aspect of ordinary funeral rites had been ignored. Catastrophes among the living, as with cholera or other illness striking numbers of people, have also been blamed upon some recently dead person whose corpse can be disinterred and treated in some final way so as to end its supposed malevolent activity. Often the treatment lies in driving a stake through its heart or in cremating the corpse. A great deal of folklore over the broad vampire tradition can be and has been explained in rational terms describing the decomposition of the body, including its exudation of fluids that can make it appear as though it has drunk blood and the making of noises through body-rupture through pressure of gases (Barber 1988).

## Fear Abolished

While traditional religious belief helps many offset any such fear of death through the compensatory hope of a destiny beyond the grave, there is one particularly interesting group of people who reckon to have personal experience of that world and who have attained both a sense of absolute certainty and a sense of peace resulting from their experience. Here I do not have in mind the Spiritualists mentioned in earlier chapters whose afterlife belief comes from séances, but from those who have been medically resuscitated after, apparently, being dead and who report what have come to be called near-death experiences. The contrast between the séance parlour and the hospital resuscitation room could hardly be greater and yet the effects may be similar.

Numerous reports exist of what Raymond Moody called near-death experiences (NDE). Typically, though accounts do vary, some people whose hearts have stopped and who, yet, have been brought back to conscious life through medical intervention, tell of a journey through a tunnel of light, an encounter with a kindly figure who may or may not be surrounded by family and friends of the 'deceased' person (Moody 1975). That figure informs the person that the time for entry into that world has not yet arrived and that he or she needs to return to their earthly existence. Accordingly they travel back and find themselves 'alive' again. It is precisely their sense of personal conviction that death is no longer problematic that typifies many of these people. Their sense of certainty is given voice and they are often prepared to encourage others who may fear death. There are even some groups formed by those who have not had the experience themselves but who gain encouragement from those who have. Time will tell if such groups of the very late twentieth century will develop into some kind of religious-like movement.

Somewhat analogous to near-death experiences are out of the body experiences (OBEs), which some people have also experienced during medical procedures. Typically they find themselves looking down upon their physical body as it is being operated upon, and upon recovery they speak of aspects of what went on around them. Some see such experiences as a clear proof of the existence of a separate life-centre or soul that can exist independent of the body.

Though near-death and out of the body experiences gained a great deal of explicit attention in the 1980s and 90s, occasional examples can be found in different sorts of much earlier and different kinds of literature. Bede's eighth-century *History of the English Church and People*, for example, tells of the monk Fursey who, when unconscious, was taken on a journey into heavenly realms where he 'saw not only the great joys of the blessed, but the amazing struggles of evil spirits' (1955: 168). He even suffered burns from one enduring fiery torments in the afterlife, burns that 'left a permanent and visible scar on his shoulder and jaw, and in this strange way his body afforded visible evidence of the inward sufferings of his soul' (1955: 170). This may be one kind of example of what would, in the life of St Francis of Assisi in the thirteenth century, become the stigmata, the marks of the suffering and death of Jesus imprinted upon or manifest through the body of this believer. In the twentieth century Padre Pio, a much-venerated Italian Catholic priest, was one of the best-known stigmatics. There is a peculiar power of death transcendence evident in him through the symbolic power of a priest – whose hands bleed from the stigmatic wounds – standing at the altar to offer the sacrifice of the Mass, which involves a kind of re-offering of the death of Jesus for the sins of the world. Such a figure helps contradict the fear of death and fosters the faithful in their belief in Christ and eternity, for there is a sense in which these Christian stigmatists express a kind of 'death in the body experience'.

Other cultures, too, offer numerous cases. One such is described by Farnham Rehfisch for the Mambila of Nigeria. He tells of a woman who apparently died and whose journey into the afterlife involved a meeting with the ancestors in a kind of heavenly village in which everything was in excellent condition and included large quantities of goods only then becoming available in Nigeria. When the ancestors learned that she still had young children they chided her for leaving the children and 'said that it was a mistake to have let her die. The next thing she knew, she awoke on her bed' (Rehfisch 1969: 309).

In terms of the history of religion both near-death and out of the body experiences share some similarity with experiences related to the making of shamans, those specialists believed to be mediators between the realm of the living and of the otherworld, able to travel between the two and bring some succour to the living. The medical context adds a scientific frame to the hope for death transcendence and shows how the human engagement with death is ever-changing in form.

# Chapter 8

# Purposeful and Useless Death

This final chapter looks at different kinds of death in terms of their apparent purposefulness or uselessness, for death has long been one of the most powerful of all natural symbols, a medium for ever invested with distinctive social meaning. The corpse itself is seldom left socially neutral, some object to be discarded. It is almost always invested with particular cultural interpretation, bearing meanings in its death just as in life. In a more abstract sense, too, 'death' is deeply invested with significance and is usually set within some mythology or theology that seeks to explain the meaning of existence. One contemporary paradox affecting death and corpses in many secularized westernized contexts is that explanations of death have moved to the periphery of society's active concern, prompting the question of whether death may be rendered practically redundant. Even to ponder that question is to raise the profound religious and philosophical issue of the value of a life that sees but little meaning in death. That is not to say that a marginalized sense of death could not carry much significance, but it is to note the changing nature of individual and social life in relation to death. Might it be easier than one might have imagined for new interpretations of death and life to replace theological explanations that have served well for millennia but which are no longer accepted? What are the dynamics involved in such changes?

Theories concerning the cosmos as developed by physicists and astronomers operate on time scales that render an individual's life and death insignificant. Biology and genetics, by contrast, stress the survival of bodily features but hardly engage with the meaning of a person's life. Psychology and psychiatry go some way in handling those personal dynamics but at a much reduced level of explanation: they are more therapeutic and deal with how we cope in life rather than concern themselves with ultimate issues. Amidst this absence of ultimacy ethics has appeared very rapidly as one substitute for religious explanations of life. Central to the force of contemporary ethics lies the prime issue of human rights and the worth of individual right to life. The strong this-worldly focus of secular ethics has been complemented by a variety of reflections on life and death produced as much by bereaved people trying to make sense of life as by any theologian, scientist or philosopher. Partnering this rise in ethics has been an equal emergence of interest in a broad sense of 'spirituality'. As we have argued in previous chapters, the balance of opinion seems to be shifting the 'meaning of life' and therefore the 'meaning of death' from some form of ultimate afterlife to either a personal and interpersonal comfort zone of private satisfaction or to an ongoing this-worldliness concerned with the future of the race and the ecological future of the planet.

In this final chapter we reflect further on some of these issues, not only with an eye on the fact of physical death which is a constant guarantor that it cannot be left without some significance but also on the prevailing import of death in parts of the world where it remains far more visible as a medium open to exploitation.

## Power of Death

Politically speaking, power is evident in control over the human body, with the right to kill or not to kill jealously guarded by the state. Murderers, who have detracted from the welfare of their society or enemies actively attacking it, have traditionally been subjected to capital punishment or death in warfare. The execution of a serial killer removes a source of malevolence from society and affirms the very nature of justice, just as, through warfare, a state extends its power for the welfare of its members or the political goals of its leadership. In the second half of the twentieth century, however, numerous democratic countries have removed the death penalty on their assumption that its existence detracts from their notion of civilization and the way in which violence should be handled within society. These changing attitudes to death make the waging of war all the more problematic and highlight the problem of terrorism, since terrorism is the act of imposing death upon members of a society within their own territory and not upon some field of battle. This was one reason why the terrorist attack upon New York on 11 September 2001 was so devastating. Indeed, the emergence of terrorism, especially in the latter part of the twentieth century, introduced a distinctive element within the history of death in that, all political, religious and economic issues apart, these apparently random killings provided a focus for that fear which can easily be the shadow-side of the sense of security that had been cultivated amongst relatively rich citizens in settled political societies.

## Warfare

Behind both warfare and terrorism, the human animal cannot avoid the description of being a killer. While avoiding the arguments as to whether this is more of a male than female characteristic and whether it is genetically rooted in our primate past – given, for example, the fact that some chimpanzees actively engage in hunting and killing their own kind – the fact remains that war is a constant feature of human history. War is nothing less than a socially sanctioned imposition of death upon an enemy. It is an aspect of human behaviour all too readily overlaid with moral value, as in the notion of 'just war' theory in Christian moral philosophy. Thomas Aquinas in the thirteenth century, for example, argued that Christians could conduct war if pursued on the authority of the monarch, with a just cause and with participants having a proper intention. Already, from the beginning of the twelfth century, the Crusades of Christendom against Islamic control of the Holy Land and its prized sites witnessed a distinctive kind of Christian warfare that included barbarity in the name of religion. As a militarized form of pilgrimage believed to bring religious benefit to participants, the Crusades echoed something of the ideal of the martyr originating in the persecution of the earliest Christian generations whose martyr-graves often became sites of churches and worship. The spiritual benefits of death under persecution became subtly transformed into the benefit of death gained in battle. Similar ideas exist in Islamic notions of defending the faith even if it involves a self-prompted death as part of sacred warfare.

Though Christian states would, in later centuries, battle with each other, as both world wars attest, differences of religious culture could always fire additional military zeal. Ongoing relations between Christian and Islamic countries attest to this even into the twenty-first century. The American sense of itself as a Christian democracy is far from insignificant in its responsive aggression against Iraq. In its day the Nazi war machine and its 'ultimate solution' of destroying the Jews and some other selected groups through concentration camps, gas chambers and crematoria offered a classic example of ethnic-religion used to define an enemy. At the bar both of international law and of common human morality, that act of Nazi genocide stands condemned.

While a death is a death as far as the person killed is concerned, the 'value' of that death depends upon the perspective of a society, even of a world community. So, for example, the use of the atomic bomb by the USA in Japan towards the close of the Second World War was an extreme example of political power used to destroy human bodies and from the American standpoint was a positive use of power over a civilian population in order to bring a political regime to surrender and prevent even greater loss of life. To those annihilated and maimed, however, such force could hardly be deemed just. Yet, while Hiroshima and Nagasaki stand as twentieth-century symbols of power against enemy bodies, they seldom attract the same interpretation as does the Holocaust of the Jews. This may be partly due to the human predicament emphasized by Jay Winter who concluded his historical analysis of grief and memorials in the First World War by saying that the search for 'meaning' after the catastrophic battle sites of mass death of the First War was 'bad enough' but that, 'after Auschwitz and Hiroshima' this became 'infinitely more difficult' (Winter 1995: 228). Quite a different interpretation has argued that the USA engages in warfare and the blood-loss of its own soldiers as a kind of self-sacrificial means of uniting the disparate worlds of the USA around its President and flag (Marvin and Ingle 1999). Be that as it may, there is a human response, a focused poignancy, an evocative potency, that comes from images of starved, punished and maimed bodies. Photographic records of suffering individuals, whether in Japan or Vietnam, provoke responses amongst people who seek a sense of civilization in which dying and dead bodies are not the measure of victory.

## Genocide

In this context it is important not to limit our concern with world or international wars but also to consider the fact of genocide. Since the combination of identity and destiny is a major key to understanding attitudes to death, genocide easily takes its place as the most extreme form of this combination when framed by political power. Identity and destiny shape nationalism and tribalism, giving them a profound sense of importance and of a right to destroy those defined as the enemy. On the larger canvas the human species displays a considerable tendency towards warfare and antagonism in the drive for power. The genocide that took place in Rwanda in 1994 presents a stark example in which close to a million people belonging to the Tutsi tribal group were killed by those of Hutu identity. Though much marked in 2004 as a decade on from the event, most countries, including the United Nations Organization, did nothing to prevent the massacre, nor the even greater numbers slaughtered in Rwanda's neighbouring Congo areas. Certainly, it is right to describe the Rwandan deaths as slaughter given the body-penetrating torture employed. Hutu and Tutsi had lived together for a very long time, some had even intermarried, but a series of political shifts of power seemed to catalyse a longstanding identity difference between them grounded in the 'Hamitic Hypothesis': the idea that the Tutsi were, really, of quite different descent from the Hutu. Missionaries had espoused this pseudo-historical genealogy which gave the Tutsi a belief that they came from the biblical character Ham, the (albeit cursed) grandson of Noah. Viewed by many Europeans in Africa as superior to the Hutu, the Tutsi claim to superiority was reacted to through genocide. Christopher Taylor's account of these killings subtly shows how indigenous symbolism worked its way out through forms of torture and death, but he also reminds us of many other contexts of genocide (Taylor 1999). The killing of native peoples in North and South America, Australia, Tasmania and beyond has involved enormous amounts of suffering and death in the name of colonialism and the importing of a 'higher' civilization. Religion combines with politics in identity wars and conflict over territory whether in Northern Ireland's Protestant–Catholic conflict between Royalist and Nationalist or the ongoing engagements of Jews, Muslims and Christians in the Middle East. Within Europe the eight thousand or so Muslims killed by Orthodox Christian Bosnian Serbs in 1995 present a specific example of massacre of tremendous scale amongst people who had also previously lived as neighbours. When former US President Clinton unveiled a memorial to this devastation in September 2003 he hinted at the fact that there was now a possibility for peace in the Balkans but that there was no guarantee of it. Once more the sense of fragility of peace demonstrates the human potential for killing in the name of one's own prior claim to dominance and truth.

## Violence at Heart

One of the deepest problems in the history of death is the problem of violence and the ease with which people and societies kill. We have seen this expressed in the Genesis myth of Cain and Abel; it also appears in Greek tragedy and well beyond. It is not insignificant that when Sigmund Freud developed his own 'mythology' of psychoanalysis to explain the human condition he constructed his own myth of the killing of the primal father by his sons in order to get at the protected women. In his *Totem and Taboo* he reckons the very notion of 'culture' to emerge 'born' at that very moment, partnering as it did the simultaneous emergence both of the incest taboo and the guilt arising from patricide (1960 [1913]). This sense of intrinsic violence has been pursued by others, especially by René Girard who not only sees violence as lying at the heart of society but also regards religion, especially sacrifice, as the prime means of channelling and controlling its potentially devastating power (1977).

## Disasters

From quite a different direction natural disasters, sometimes allied with political maladministration, have also taken their toll on human life, with starvation and death becoming distinctive features of international political life in the second half of the twentieth century. The 1980s response to the Ethiopian Famine in the form of the Live Aid concert focused on Bob Geldof was a good example of an event that brought together hundreds of pop music stars from across the world linked by immense international television technology and reaching more people at one time than, probably, had ever been achieved before. This was, in a sense, the first wonder of the international pop music world and was a direct response to the reality of starvation and death revealed to the world in picture form and responded to in a form of entertainment which took that word into a new level of moral significance.

The death of Diana, Princess of Wales, in 1997 witnessed the next most dramatic engagement of the mass media with a human tragedy. This time it was sharply individual, focused on a high-profile individual rather than on an anonymous population. The ritual occasion of her very public funeral elicited what the media constantly described as an 'outpouring' of emotion and discussed in terms of the uniqueness of the massed response. In actual historical fact, very similar public reactions had taken place within Britain over the deaths and funerals of numerous prominent persons, from the Duke of Wellington to David Livingstone to Edward VII to Winston Churchill. These and other royal, political and military figures of Great Britain have been admirably documented and analysed by John Wolffe (2000). Such deaths, whether quite sudden and unexpected or long anticipated, nevertheless led to large public gatherings and a display of emotion. What is obvious in them all is the way in which the deceased person is used as a means of reflecting upon prime values of a society.

Such 'great deaths', as Wolffe describes them, illustrate the way in which values are embodied in and through someone's life. It is when they die that eulogies and newspapers, sermons and television elucidate those values and praise them in the lives that have been lived. This reflects on a large scale and national stage much of what often occurs locally in the words of appreciation of a life that accompany most deaths. But, with the great and the good, it is not simply a case of 'not speaking ill of the dead' or finding something good to say about them even if it takes some doing, but an issue of placing their life within the historical flow of society. Here a relatively limited number of themes come to the fore, especially those of dedicated service and self-sacrifice, values that are crucial for the well-being of society at large. They can also be occasions on which negative values can be highlighted, especially in ideas of betrayal or disrespect as emerged in the case of Diana, Princess of Wales. Much was made by the media at large of the view that she had been negatively treated by the Royal Family. Such comment and, indeed, the way death at large is discussed for national figures is much influenced by the deep cultural grammar of emotional value that exists in a country, not least that provided by Christianity.

Indeed, the history of most Christian-influenced cultures has cherished the death of Christ, investing it with the highest significance as a sacrifice of one who was deemed to be divine, dying for the ultimate salvation of humanity. That strong positive element, already detailed in chapter 1, can also be matched by the negative theme of betrayal as and when it might be appropriate. The death of dedicated believers in contexts of martyrdom was also accorded high praise and this was extended to the death of soldiers fighting for the faith or, as the twentieth century came to express it, fighting for their countries against evil regimes. The biblical text from St John's Gospel that includes the words 'Greater love has no man than this, that a man lay down his life for his friends' (John 15: 13) itself came to be adopted as an inscription upon thousands of war memorials. High praise is also accorded to the death of parents and others who have given unstintingly of their care and time for the advantage of their children and community. Most ordinary people are also, if at all possible, praised after their death in order to set their life within a worthwhile context. Beyond such 'ordinary' death can be found that of people on the very fringe of society, exemplified, for example, by people who live on the streets and die in a doorway, sick and alone. Modern societies will ensure that they are given a funeral but it is likely to be an extremely small and brief affair. The purpose of such a death reflects what might be deemed the relative purposelessness of the life once lived since, frequently, the value of a death matches the value of a life in the eyes of society at large.

## Baby-Death

To speak of deaths as 'purposeful' or 'useless' is to highlight the value accorded to them. But such distinctions can become problematic in cases such as still-births and apparently untimely death through accident or illness. In many societies still-births and even the death of infants have often been passed over with a minimum of ceremony or have not even been marked at all. In today's rich societies people have few children and pregnancies are largely planned, with children being given a firm identity while still in the womb. Such benefits of advanced technology as ultrasound scanning and the like make baby-deaths more significant than ever before. Similarly with the death of young people due to accident or some misfortune when relatives devotedly seek the cause so that, as the popularly powerful expression has it, 'it may never happen again'. In this way what is, otherwise, a meaningless death is given some semblance of potential purpose. Something similar happens when organs from an accidental death of a young person are given to seriously ill people. Where younger people die from illness it is not uncommon for their family to become committed to support groups for similarly bereaved people, often with the intention of fostering research into that particular fatal illness. This, too, seeks to bring a degree of meaning to the death in societies where risk to life is much less than in many underdeveloped societies or in the history of their own society. Different social classes or occupational groups also possess a varying sense of risk in life since existence is, generally, much 'safer' for the rich than for the poor.

One of the tragedies of today's world is that death is treated as a cause of concern in some contexts while in others the warfare and sickness killing millions pass practically unnoticed. The relative worth of life differs, not least in terms of how the media decide to comment or not. Indeed, a significant aspect of the presence of death in the early twenty-first century is that of the media and their power to advertise or ignore as they see fit. For them newsworthiness replaces any sense of life-worthiness or the degree of risk of life and limb.

## Suicide – Euthanasia

One category of death that is particularly problematic for relatively 'risk-free' societies is suicide. At the individual, family and community level a suicide often prompts much soul-searching and discussion of why the person may have killed him or herself. While there is, sometimes, an apparently obvious reason, on many occasions there is none, which calls into question the reasonableness of life itself. The problematic nature of suicide is evident in Christianity since, by about the sixth century, it was deplored and led to the custom of not burying suicides in consecrated cemeteries, even though some sympathetic clergy may have done so. Suicide became a sin; it even passed into secular law and it was not until 1961, for example, that it ceased to be an offence in England. However, even by the seventeenth century the English poet and Dean of St Paul's Cathedral, John Donne, was reflecting seriously on the impropriety of denouncing suicides (Clebsch 1983). For Donne the mercy and grace of God should not be overlooked, nor should it be so easily assumed that all people sought self-preservation at all costs, a view that was largely followed in the major stream of Catholic tradition which also views God as the master of life and humans as stewards of it. Suicide contradicts both the proper love one should have for oneself and the bonds of community that exist between people. Even so, Catholic teaching does not render suicide meaningless. Not only does it offer the possibility that a person may be psychologically disturbed or in a state of diminished responsibility but also, 'by ways known to him alone, God can provide the opportunity for salutary repentance', with the Church also prepared to pray for such individuals. Philosophers, too, from Plato to David Hume and Albert Camus, have reflected upon the place of freedom of thought and action implicated in suicide. The influential American anthropologist Ruth Benedict dwelt much upon death and when she thought about her own she 'wanted to be alert to this next experience in life' (Modell 1984: 311). One of her ideals was of balance and fulfilment, prompting her 'wishing for death' but not being in favour of suicide because it was a 'cheap way' of attaining the otherwise desirable goal.

While, at the individual level, suicide may be unfathomable, at a social level some degree of regularity may be observed. This was an important point made by Emile Durkheim's *Suicide* published in 1897, which contributed enormously to developing a field of suicide studies. He suggested three forms of suicide, egoistic – in which persons were insufficiently networked into society, altruistic – in which people could not cope with the intense social control surrounding them, and anomic suicide in which someone is overwhelmed by the powerful organization of society, not least its economic power. Though much criticized and with many later forms being suggested by others, Durkheim's work stresses the social factors framing any individual predisposition. Van Gennep briefly notes the significance of suicide and follows an earlier scheme of R. Lasch who identified four conditions: where suicide was treated like other forms of death, where it was rewarded, as with warriors or widows, where it left a person to wander between the realms of the living and the dead, and finally where suicide was punished in the next life (van Gennep 1960: 161 citing Lasch 1900: 110–15).

Major issues of the late twentieth century that are set to develop a great deal are those of assisted suicide and euthanasia, for there is a growing body of opinion that sees a 'right to die' as part of one's human rights. The alternative view that God alone is responsible for giving and taking life closely resembles its secular variant, viz., that society possesses that right. Some couch the argument against assisted suicide in terms of the slippery slope whereby either doctors will wish to terminate the lives of some or else the very old or infirm, already alluded to in terms of inhabiting a 'non-space', will feel obliged to die lest they be a burden upon their relatives.

As increasing numbers of people think of themselves as consumers possessing a great deal of choice and self-determination they are likely to apply that elective attitude to their own life and death. Just as death rites are likely to move further away from religious control so, in time, it is likely that decisions to live or die, especially in contexts of interminable suffering and a sense of indignity, will become more personal.


## Offending Deaths

Despite our opening thoughts on the marginalizing of death, some of the tragic deaths just mentioned do highlight the importance of death as an expression of social values and can be interpreted through what I have called the theory of offending death. Indeed, it may even be that these high-profile deaths assume their powerful symbolic role precisely because of the relative social insignificance of thousands of individual experiences of bereavement.

I define 'offending deaths' as those that cause many people within a society to join together in a mass response of anger and disgust in protest against the killing of people deemed to be innocent victims and in calling for reparation from those in positions of authority. Offending death quite literally offends against prime social values and causes a deep, gut-level, reaction. What is particularly significant about offending deaths is that the very authorities that stand as guardians of public life seem to be implicated in the deaths or to be the very cause of the deaths. What is more, such deaths take a variety of forms.

The case of the Ethiopian famine and the Live Aid response mentioned above was a typical example. Here the death of 'innocent children' focused the issue, with politicians pinpointed as inactive in the face of such human tragedy. A widely televised confrontation between Bob Geldof and Britain's Prime Minister, Mrs Margaret Thatcher, brought ordinary human fellow-feeling into sharp contrast with the apparently relentless face of political process perceived as unresponsive to tragedy.

An even more forceful example is that of 'The White March' which took place in Belgium in 1996, when hundreds of thousands of ordinary citizens marched in Brussels in protest against paedophile murders that seemed to be going without appropriate levels of police and government response. There was talk of people in high positions being involved in some way, with the individual widely believed to be responsible not being brought to account rapidly enough. Years later this case continued to be problematic, with a small and unofficial 'shrine' of memorial flowers and pictures of children being placed at one of the entrances to the absolutely immense civic administrative hall in Brussels, and not removed for fear of further public aggravation.

In England on 30 August 2002 some 2,000 people gathered in Ely Cathedral for a service commemorating the lives of two ten-year-old girls, Holly Wells and Jessica Chapman, who had been murdered by the caretaker of their school. Considerable national interest was taken in this case, from the time these young girls went missing, through to the discovery of their bodies and on into the final trial of the murderer. Ultimately, in April 2004, the caretaker's house at the school was demolished to remove the constant scene of the crime from the view of villagers. These murders offer a clear case of a person abusing a 'caretaker' role; one who should – albeit in a relatively limited social sense – uphold basic values inverted them as a murderer. The girls were so obviously victims, and their death expressive of social evil. One consequence involved a serious tightening-up of checks on teachers and others connected with children to ensure they had no record of offences against children.

The death of Diana, Princess of Wales, though quite different in the form of death, prompted its own mass popular response of the highest order, with a similarly high level of calling into question the responsibility of various groups of people in positions of authority. Conspiracy theories surrounding the fatal car crash caused the Monarchy itself to change some of its attitudes and customs, while the media, whose reporters had dogged the Princess in her private as well as public life, were also called to account. She was depicted as a victim who had suffered an unjust death because of the improper actions of those charged with social responsibility.

Other cases could also be discussed and would, for example, embrace concentration camp deaths during the Second World War's Holocaust which, although circumstances did not produce any massed reaction at the time, has subsequently evoked a universal acknowledgement of wrong. Yet, by contrast and as already mentioned earlier, the literal holocaust caused by the USA's nuclear attacks upon Hiroshima and Nagasaki as a move to bring the Second World War to an end by bringing Japan to defeat is seldom treated in this negative way.

Hiroshima and Nagasaki do pinpoint, however, the strategic use of death as part of political and international life. Warfare itself seems to be an intrinsic element of human social life and its prime medium is death. In this sense the history of warfare offers one of the clearest streams of the history of death: of death as a strategic weapon in the human drive for power. That power can be described as either good or evil and depends upon one's own political, philosophical or religious standpoint. Hitler's use of military might, or Stalin's forceful control of his civilian population, can be interpreted as quite unlike the US or British use of force in the twentieth or, indeed, twenty-first century, but the fact remains that it is the ultimate cost of death – to both civilian and military personnel – that pays for implementing political ideals.

Though often ignored or marginalized by the media and political world of western democracies, almost unbelievable atrocities and large-scale slaughter have occurred and are occurring as the twentieth century ends and its successor begins. Parts of the Congo in Africa and, more advertised, the attempted genocide in Rwanda in 1994 with, as we have already discussed, perhaps as many as a million dead, have witnessed the slaughter and maiming of people as part of political campaigns and drives for power.

## Illness and Death

By sharp contrast to crowd murder, one feature of later twentieth- and early twenty-first-century life in developed societies has been the growth in self-help support groups amongst individuals suffering from particular illnesses or terminal diseases, and also amongst bereaved families. Far from submitting to the inevitability of their condition, these pursue some advantage through mutual support and by seeking to alleviate the circumstances that bring about the cause of illness. The response to the tragic and accidental death of a son or daughter can involve parents setting up funds to support the favoured activity of their lost child. All of these circumstances help bring a degree of meaning-through-action to circumstances that could, otherwise, lead to a sense of meaningless despair.

## The Future of Death

Human beings make their world meaningful. Far from being an abstract and philosophical idea, 'meaning' is a practical hallmark of human society. From archaeological remains to the architecture of today, people stamp their presence upon the world, not least when it comes to death. Time after time, biological death is given its cultural significance as the neutral message carrier of the inert corpse allows the living to use it to express their own thoughts and views of destiny. The way the corpse is treated, dressed and handled allows both retrospective and prospective views of the dead to be expressed by the living. Retrospectively the corpse reflects its former status and relations in the world when dressed and buried with objects expressing its former identity and surrounded by messages of love from kin and friends. Prospectively it carries hopes of what lies beyond. Such past status and future hope were never more clearly expressed than by Egyptian royalty who, in their treasure-trove tombs, displayed their former wealth just as they were also spell-bound for their future existence amidst the heavens. But such an emphasis of past and future is not everywhere as balanced as with the great pharaohs. We have already seen in chapter 3 how cremation ritual accompanied a secular shift in thought in many European countries. Where the fullness of human existence comes to be seen in terms of this world and not some heaven, so the dead body symbolizes this life rather than the life-beyond.

## Christian Eternal Life

To Albert Schweitzer (1875–1965) and C. S. Lewis (1893–1963), introduced earlier as Christian thinkers addressing the fear of death, we now return as individuals who may be seen to represent two ends of a spectrum of Christian thought on death.

Schweitzer even shades into what some will see as a more secular view.

Traditional Christianity saw this world as a preparation for heaven. Many Christians have viewed Jesus as a victim whose unjust death evokes a response of devotion, loyalty and self-sacrificial service to humanity exemplified in Schweitzer's own medical mission in Africa. For many, Christ's resurrection also promised heavenly joy while a darker stream of spirituality emphasized hell as the afterlife alternative for the ultimately wicked, with purgatory as a necessary preparatory phase of moral cleansing for the large majority of souls. But times are changing and the widespread discussion about tradition, modernity and postmodernity affects traditional beliefs a great deal. The eighteenth century began an erosion of ecclesiastically controlled power over people rooted in the fear of eternity and the nineteenth century extended this as hell declined still further. Beyond Christian fundamentalism few address themselves to hell; indeed, even heaven receives little attention by comparison with a this-worldly focus on the ethics of justice and a desire for self- and social fulfilment.

Though easily spoken of as a single entity, 'Christianity' is, actually, a multiple reality. Traditional Catholic thought, for its part, sees a profound moral and psychological logic in purgatory, while Protestants see it as a denial of the full salvation brought about by Christ and assume that resurrection will, instantaneously, provide any change demanded before sinners meet God. Traditional Christians, whatever their denomination, maintain a fundamental belief in an ultimate heavenly afterlife whether through a bodily resurrection, an immortal soul or some idea of the dead being held in the divine memory – much as a message is within a computer. To deviate from a 'life everlasting' would be an absurd and unfaithful deviation from the Christian message. Not all Christians are traditionalist, however, with some liberals preferring not to speak of life after death but of a deep sense of 'eternal life' in the here and now. In Schweitzer's case this quality of contemporary experience is taken as an experience that removes any fear of death or over one's future non-existence. The resurrection of Jesus is, in this perspective, likely to be interpreted as an experience of the apostles that brought them to a sense of new purpose in life, one shared in a community and expressed through an ethical life driven by a sense of love. For the traditional believer this pale reflection of belief betrays both biblically and ecclesiastically rooted Christianity, with some adopting extremely modern means of explaining their belief, including scientific notions of matter, energy and its transformation, but always with the intention of retaining a self and relationships in some future form of existence. Conservatives feel that their sense of the love of God must mean that God will not allow death to extinguish this precious bond and that God will, somehow, cause the individual to live again beyond death. This same argument from love and for love then explains that human relationships must be continued after death because without relationships the human identity is bare and the self a nothingness. The next step in this argument is that some form of body will be necessary for these relationships to take place since we only know each other through our bodies.

As we intimated at the beginning of this chapter, however, increasing numbers of people in western societies do not believe in this traditional Christian version of life after death. Secular movements stress the absurdity and illusory nature of afterlife beliefs, while some nature-related individuals prefer notions of reincarnation. In many respects the secularist and the liberal Christian share a view on a this-worldly purpose of life. The Christian, however, is still committed to some notion of the community of God as a domain of justice, peace and love in whose achievement the churches will play a major role. Everything depends on perspective and the base or community from which one approaches these important questions.

## Death's Margins

Given this diversity, it looks as though death rites will, increasingly, take a dual path. Traditional Christian, Muslim, Hindu or other religious ways will develop under their own ideas of an afterlife, while some religious believers, along with secularists, will develop this-worldly forms of celebration and memorial. Already there exist a small but growing number of organizations and individuals offering such this-worldly funeral rites. This is likely to increase and could do so quite dramatically if and when funeral directors take it upon themselves to advertise such possibilities. But funeral directors are amongst the more, and often most, conservative of agencies, not least because a relatively standardized format of funeral is easiest to manage and least likely to go wrong. Problematically, the clergy are amongst the relatively uncontrolled variables with which the undertaker has to deal and to bring the rite itself under the immediate control of the funeral director would be advantageous in that respect. It is equally likely that increasing numbers of undertakers will recognize the value of a degree of niche-marketing to families seeking a high degree of individuality and involvement in the proceedings. These two positions of high and low control each offer distinctive financial possibilities in dealing with bereaved people.

## Age and Death

Bereavement questions the meaningfulness of life because it questions the significance of those human relationships in which people invest a great degree of energy. As people live longer than ever before it is likely that some will be increasingly marginalized by their younger relatives caught up in hectic life-activities and deemed the 'significant' people of the world. The death of the very old, perhaps already peripheral in homes with

other old people, will become increasingly irrelevant. If technology continues to advance, society-enhancing expertise is likely
to be grasped and developed by the young in a society that
inverts the age–respect values of traditional societies in which
wisdom accrued through long years of experience. Accordingly,
the death of the young or the very young, by contrast, will be
deemed a shame. Young children and, even more so, young
adults who possess extensive networks of significance will be
mourned intensively.

## Hopeless Non-Places

Against that background we take the depiction of three ideal
types of memorial place and of hope sketched in chapter 6 and
now add a fourth, the 'hopeless non-place'. Francis Fukuyama's
*Our Posthuman Future* reflects earlier American views that 'the
fear of death is one of the most abiding human passions'. He
develops and frames this in the 'national nursing home scenario'
accounting for the old-age category of post 80-year-olds (2002:
69). He ponders the possibility of these pointless and lonely old
people devoid of those active commitments and obligations to
others that make life worth living. They live in a society where
death will have come to be seen 'not as a natural and inevitable
aspect of life, but a preventable evil like polio or measles' (2002:
71). But, he asks, will that 'unendingly empty life not appear
simply unbearable?' Or, in our present terms, will not such life
be hopeless? If we add to this view Marc Augé's development of
Michel de Certeau's notion of 'non-place', a powerful scenario
develops. In non-places people are in transit, exiled from home
and missing intense relationships. Airport lounges, motorway
service areas and the like typify such non-places: full of signs of
where to go and what to do but devoid of reference to individuals.
As users, we know we are just passing through. These non-
places hardly compare with our eschatological, retrospective and

ecological types of place and of hope; they do not carry 'monuments as testimonies and reminders' (Augé 1992: 70). Are such non-places merely the intersections of significant places through which we have to travel today, or do they typify something of a real lifestyle encroaching upon much of life? And if so, what would that mean for death-style?

Does this indicate that the preservation of life into old age will produce a generation of decreasing identity with little hope and living only in non-places? And if so, what would that mean for the dynamics of memorial sites? Fukuyama and Malinowski present challenging issues of place and hope. As we have already seen, for Malinowski hope is the desire to survive and to have a sense that life is worth living despite the pain of grief. But hope, itself, may change its content. Are one's attitudes towards a ten-year-old the same as towards a centenarian? Is 'hope' the same in each case? And what of the locales in which these individuals are set? Are hope and the nursery, hope and school, hope and church, hope and home the same as hope and the nursing home? Here the dynamics of particular locations and the economics underpinning them become significant and hint at variation. While many may feel allured by retirement cruises, they are seldom so attracted by homes for the ageing and ultimately senile.

## 2020 Time and Vision

In an intellectual vision presented as a dream at the close of his instructively titled *Spaces of Hope*, David Harvey described in some detail how society will be organized in an optimistic and hopeful world of 2020. He tells how the 2020 world treats death with dignity, with a great variety of rites that see the spirits of the dead prompting the living to take stock of their lives. His vision is, however, brought short as he wakes up in the Baltimore of 1998. Unfortunately, he awakes just before telling us what the living actually do with their dead; where do they put them? Do they end in one of Foucault's 'heterotopias' – a place quite different in value from others in its society? – we do not know (Harvey 2000: 184). We are left with an ideal type of hope but not with its location.

The less the dead are feared, the less extensive are the rites performed for their removal. Where persons have been influential, the longer and fuller tend to be their funeral ceremonies and, where appropriate, their installation in the other world. The influential take more replacing than a 'no-body', especially when dying in responsible posts. By contrast, those who die many years after relinquishing high office are much less feted. Those now in power may hardly know them and see little point in making a great show of the death, except in so far as it is polite and proper so to do. In ordinary social life, too, the death by sudden heart attack of a family's main breadwinner who may, also, be an influential person at work or in leisure circles is more marked than the death of an aged and long-retired person who never wielded any wide social influence at all. There is little to fear from the powerless when dead, just as when they were alive. Unless society comes to appreciate the very old in some currently unanticipated sense it is unlikely that their death will prompt much response. 'A quiet funeral' can be a polite way of saying that it was the closing of an uneventful life or a now-forgotten career.

## The World's Death

What then of the future? My death, yours, and the death of those to whom we are attached, as well as the masses unknown to us, lie on a sliding scale of relevance. What is tragedy for me may be of concern to you and of irrelevance to most others. And beyond our personal deaths stands the death of the world. Indeed, there is a sense in which these echo each other, even though the link is hardly ever expressed precisely because the time scale leaves us thoughtless. Still, the earth will die and so will all life on it, whether through heat or cold. Contemporary concerns with ecology and global warming are, in the face of cosmic failure, petty in the extreme. Their apparent importance only highlights our commitment to survival. While some religious believers pin their hopes on a heaven in another dimension or even on some form of transformed earth, these beliefs are increasingly unpersuasive to many modern minds.

When it comes to the meaning of life, human beings live strange lives. Day by day, society functions on values and beliefs that, at one moment, seem so solid and, at another, can dissolve into emptiness. Grief can produce that switch, as can philosophical reflection or loss of faith. Politicians weave their webs of apparent relevance, despite our knowing that much of it is self-concern. Religious leaders, often with the profoundest sincerity, portray realms of ultimate significance that some accept and others see as imaginary. Yet all live, and the drive for meaning impels us to live creatively. As social animals our sense of life as players in the cosmic game is potentially powerful in challenging us to live knowing that we will die. The history of death is a history of a kaleidoscope of sentiment: hope, fear, longing for and gratitude for love, despair at loss of endeavour, concern for our mate and offspring, whispers of a transcendent sense. These move in changing configurations, culture after culture, age after age, and within a single life the kaleidoscopic vision can transform from dark and foreboding to entrancing light.

# Bibliography

Aberbach, David (1989) *Surviving Trauma*, New Haven and London: Yale University Press.

Aberbach, David (1996) *Charisma in Politics, Religion and the Media*, London: Macmillan.

Albery, Nicholas, Gil Elliott and Joseph Elliott (1997) *The New Natural Death Handbook*, London: Rider.

Ariès, Philippe (1974) *Western Attitudes toward Death From the Middle Ages to the Present*, Boston, MA: The John Hopkins University Press.

Ariès, Philippe (1991 [1981]) *The Hour of Our Death*, Oxford: Oxford University Press.

Arriaza, Bernardo T. (1995) *Beyond Death, The Chinchorro Mummies of Ancient Chile*, Washington: Smithsonian Institution Press.

Augé, Marc (1995) *Non-Places: Introduction to an Anthropology of Supermodernity*, London: Verso.

Barber, Paul (1988) *Vampires, Burial, and Death: Folklore and Reality*, New Haven and London: Yale University Press.

Bauman, Zygmunt (1998) *Globalization*, London: Polity Press.

Baumann, Zygmunt (1992) *Mortality, Immortality*, London: Polity Press.

Bede (1955) *A History of the English Church and People*, translated and with an Introduction by Leo Sherley-Price, Harmondsworth: Penguin Books.

Blake, William (1874) *The Poems of William Blake*, London: Basil Montagu Pickering.

Bondeson, Jan (2001) *Buried Alive, The Terrifying History of our Most Primal Fear*, New York, London: W.W. Norton & Company.

Bowlby, John (1979) *The Making and Breaking of Affectional Bonds*, London: Tavistock.

Burns, Bob (1989) *Through the Whirlwind*, Nashville, TN: Oliver-Nelson Pub.

Camille, Michael (1996) *Master of Death: The Lifeless Art of Pierre Remiet, Illuminator*, New Haven and London: Yale University Press.

Camus, Albert (1960) *The Plague*, Harmondsworth: Penguin.

Carmichael, Elizabeth and Chloe Sayer (1991) *The Skeleton at the Feast: The Day of the Dead in Mexico*, London: British Museum Press.

*Catechism of the Catholic Church* (1994) London: Geoffrey Chapman.

Clebsch, William A. (ed.) (1983) *John Donne, Suicide*, Chico, CA: Scholars Press.

Cosgrove, Denis E. and Stephen Daniels (1988) *The Iconography of Landscape*, Cambridge: Cambridge University Press.

Dante, Alighieri (1984) *The Divine Comedy Vol. 1. The Inferno*, translated by Mark Musa, Harmondsworth: Penguin.

Davies, Douglas J. (1987) *Mormon Spirituality: Latter-day Saints in Wales and Zion*, Nottingham; Nottingham Series in Theology.

Davies, Douglas J. (2000) *The Mormon Culture of Salvation*, Aldershot: Ashgate.

Davies, Douglas J. (2002) *Death, Ritual and Belief*, London: Continuum.

Davies, Douglas J. and Alastair Shaw (1995) *Reusing Old Graves: A Report on Popular British Attitudes*, Crayford, Kent: Shaw and Sons Ltd.

Davies, Jon (1995) The Christian Warrior in the Twentieth Century, Lampeter: Mellen Press.

Davies, Jon (1999) *Death, Burial and Rebirth in the Religions of Antiquity*, London: Routledge.

Derbes, Anne (1996) *Picturing the Passion in Late Medieval Italy*, Cambridge: Cambridge University Press.

Durkheim, Emile (1966 [1897]) *Suicide: A Study in Sociology*, translated by John A. Spalding and George Simpson, New York: The Free Press.

Edwards, Lee MacCormack (1999) *Herkomer, A Victorian Artist*, Aldershot: Ashgate.

Eggers, Dave (2000) *A Heartbreaking Work of Staggering Genius*, London: Macmillan, Picador.

Erikson, Erik H. (1965 [1950]) *Childhood and Society*, Harmondsworth: Penguin Books.

Frazer, James G. (1913) *The Belief in Immortality and the Worship of the Dead*, London: Macmillan and Co.

Freud, Sigmund (1960 [1913]) *Totem and Taboo*, London: Routledge.

Freud, Sigmund (1975 [1920]) *Beyond the Pleasure Principle*, New York: Basic Books.

Fukuyama, Francis (2002) *Our Posthumous Future*, London: Profile Books.

Gell, Alfred (1992) *The Anthropology of Time*, Oxford: Berg.

Gennep, Arnold van (1960/1906) *The Rites of Passage*, translated by Monika B. Vizedom and Gabrielle L. Caffe, London: Routledge and Kegan Paul.

George, Andrew (1999) *The Epic of Gilgamesh*, translated and introduced by Andrew George, New York: Barnes and Noble.

Girard, René (1977) *Violence and the Sacred*, London: Johns Hopkins University Press.

Gustavson, R. F. (1986) *Leo Tolstoy: Resident and Stranger*, Princeton, NJ: Princeton University Press.

Gorer, Geoffrey (1956) 'The Pornography of Death'. In W. Phillips and P. Rahv (eds), *Modern Writing*, pp. 56–62. New York: Berkeley Press.

Harvey, David (2000) *Spaces of Hope*, Edinburgh: Edinburgh University Press, 2000.

Heidegger, Martin (1962) *Being and Time*, translated by John Macquarrie and Edward Robinson, New York: Harper and Row.

Hertz, Robert (1960 [1907]) *Death and the Right Hand*, translated by Rodney and Claudia Needham, London: Cohen and West.

Homer (1991) *The Odyssey*, translated by E. V. and D. C. H. Rieu, London: Penguin.

Jankowiak, William (ed.) (1995) *Romantic Passion*, New York: Columbia University Press.

Jones, Lindsay (2000) *The Hermeneutics of Sacred Architecture*, vol. 1, Cambridge, MA: Harvard University Press.

Jung, Carl G. (1961 [1933]) *Modern Man in Search of a Soul*, London: Routledge and Kegan Paul.

Kierkegaard, Søren (1968) *Fear and Trembling and The Sickness unto Death*, translated and with an Introduction by Walter Lowrie, Princeton, NJ: Princeton University Press.

Kübler-Ross, Elisabeth (1989 [1969]) *On Death and Dying*, London: Tavistock, Routledge.

Lasch, R. (1900) 'Die Verbleibsorte der abgeschiedened Seele der Selbstmörder', *Globus*, LXXVII, pp. 110–15.

Leach, Edmund (1961) *Rethinking Anthropology*, New York: University of London: The Athlone Press.

Lewis, C. S. (1947) *Miracles*, London: Geoffrey Bles, The Centenary Press.

Lodge, Sir Oliver (1918) *Christopher, a Study in Human Personality*, London: Cassell and Company Ltd.

MacColl, Ewan (1990) *Journeyman, an Autobiography*, London: Sidgwick and Jackson.

Marnham, Patrick (1992) *The Man Who Wasn't Maigret, A Portrait of Georges Simenon*, London: Bloomsbury.

Malinowski, Bronislaw (1974 [1948]) *Magic, Science and Religion and Other Essays*, London: Souvenir Press.

Marvin, Carolyn and David W. Ingle (1999) *Blood Sacrifice and the Nation, Totem Rituals and the American Flag*, Cambridge: Cambridge University Press.

McGinn, Bernard (1993) 'The Letter and the Spirit: Spirituality as an Academic Discipline', *Christian Spirituality Bulletin*, vol. 1, no. 2, pp. 2–9.

Metzger, Arnold (1973) *Freedom and Death*, translated by Ralph Mannheim, London: Human Context Books.

Milton, John (2000) *Paradise Lost*, London: Penguin Books.

Mims, Cedric (1998) *When We Die*, London: Robinson.

Mitford, Jessica (1963) *The American Way of Death*, New York: Simon and Schuster.

Modell, Judith (1984) *Ruth Benedict, Patterns of Life*, London: Chatto & Windus, The Hogarth Press.

Moody, Raymond A. (1975) *Life after Life: The Investigation of a Phenomenon-Survival of Bodily Death*, New York: Bantam.

Musa, Mark (1984) *Dante, The Divine Comedy Vol. 1. The Inferno*, Harmondsworth: Penguin.

Okely, Judith (1994) 'Vicarious and Sensory Knowledge of Chronology and Change, Ageing in Rural France'. In Kirsten Hatsrup and Peter Hervik (eds.) *Social Experience and Anthropological Knowledge*, London: Routledge.

Petrucci, Armando (1998) *Writing the Dead*, Stanford: Stanford University Press.

Pinckney, Darryl (1992) *High Cotton*, London: Faber and Faber.

Plato (1974) *The Republic*, translated by Desmond Lee (Second Edition, Revised), Harmondsworth: Penguin Books.

Rehfisch, Farnham (1969) 'Death, Dreams, and the Ancestors in Mambila Culture'. In Mary Douglas and Phyllis M. Kaberry (eds), *Man in Africa*, London: Tavistock Publications.

Richardson, Ruth (1987) *Death, Dissection and the Destitute*, London: Routledge and Kegan Paul.

Rowling, J. K. (1999) *Harry Potter and the Prisoner of Azkaban*, London: Bloomsbury.

Sartre, Jean Paul (1956) *Being and Nothingness*, translated by Hazel E. Barnes, New York: Philosophical Library.

Schweitzer, Albert (1974) *Reverence for Life*, London: S.P.C.K.

Shakespeare, William (1954) *William Shakespeare, The Complete Works*, (ed.) C. J. Sisson, London: Odhams Press.

Sheppy, Paul P. J. (2003) *Death Liturgy and Ritual*, vols 1 and 2, Aldershot: Ashgate.

Shotter, John (1998) 'The Dialogical nature of Our Inner Lives', *Philosophical Explorations*, no. 3, September, pp. 185–200.

Sliggers, B. C. (ed.) (1998) *Naar Het Lik: Het Nederlandse doodsportret 1500-heden*, Uitgeversmaatschappij Walburg Pers.

Stassinopoulos Huffington, Arianna (1988) *Picasso Creator and Destroyer*, New York: Simon and Schuster.

Stroebe, Wolfgang and Margaret S. Stroebe (1987) *Bereavement and Health*, Cambridge: Cambridge University Press.

Taves, Ann (1999) *Fits, Trances and Visions*, Princeton, NJ: Princeton University Press.

Taylor, Christopher C. (1999) *Sacrifice as Terror, The Rwandan Genocide of 1994*, Oxford: Berg.

Tillich, Paul (1973) *The Boundaries of Our Being*, London: Collins.

Turner, Harold W. (1979) *From Temple to Meeting House: The Phenomenology and Theology of Places of Worship*, The Hague: Mouton.

Twitchell, James B. (1981) *The Living Dead, A Study of the Vampire in Romantic Literature*, Durham, NC: Duke University Press.

Winter, Jay (1995) *Sites of Memory Sites of Mourning*, Cambridge: Cambridge University Press.

Wolffe, John (2000) *Great Deaths, Grieving, Religion, and Nationhood in Victorian and Edwardian Britain*, The British Academy: Oxford University Press.

Young, Katherine (2002) 'The Memory of the Flesh', *Body and Society*, vol. 8, no. 3, pp. 25–48.

# Index